DEAD
HEAVY
FANTASTIC

BY ROBERT FARQUHAR

Liverpool Everyman and Playhouse
Presents Dead Heavy Fantastic
By Robert Farquhar

First performed on 11 March 2011
at the Everyman Theatre, Liverpool

About the Everyman and Playhouse

Liverpool Everyman and Playhouse together make up a single engine for creative excellence, artistic adventure and audience involvement. In recent years the theatres have been on a remarkable journey, described as "a theatrical renaissance on Merseyside" Observer

An integrated programme across the two theatres has generated critical acclaim and audience growth, and has been the springboard for forward looking programmes of artist development and youth and community engagement. In Autumn 2010 more than 25,000 theatregoers watched Kim Cattrall and Jeffery Kissoon in the title roles of Janet Suzman's critically acclaimed production of *Antony and Cleopatra* at the Playhouse. Whilst at the Everyman there was a collaboration with one of the UK's pioneering theatre companies Slung Low on an *Anthology* of seven new plays by Everyman writers, performed in rep with *'Tis Pity She's A Whore*.

The Liverpool Everyman and Playhouse frequently collaborate with partners beyond Liverpool and the UK, taking work to new audiences and keeping Liverpool firmly on the national cultural map.

Current collaborations include *Oedipus* with Nottingham Playhouse, adapted and directed by Steven Berkoff, and *Roald Dahl's Twisted Tales* by Jeremy Dyson with Lyric Hammersmith and Northern Stage.

However, there is more to the theatres than simply the work on their stages. A productive Literary Department continues to nurture the next generation of Liverpool playwrights, while a wide ranging Community Department takes theatre to all corners of the city, working in partnership with schools, colleges, and youth and community groups.

In 2011 the Everyman embarks on a £28m redevelopment to replace a tumbledown former chapel with a vibrant creative hub fit for the 21st century. To register for updates on the new Everyman's plans and progress, please email ev4everyone@everymanplayhouse.com.

To find out more about the work of the Liverpool Everyman and Playhouse, both on and off stage, call 0151 709 4776 or visit www.everymanplayhouse.com.

Two great theatres. One creative heart.

Artistic Director Gemma Bodinetz
Executive Director Deborah Aydon

Liverpool Everyman and Playhouse is a registered charity No.1081229

0151 709 4776
WWW.EVERYMAN
PLAYHOUSE.COM

EVERYMAN
L I V E R P O O L
PLAYHOUSE

Credits

Cast (in alphabetical order)

Michelle Butterly	Maureen
David Carlyle	Stevie / Preacher / Young Man at Karaoke
Helen Carter	Julie / Dee / Goldfish Woman / Dawn
Stephen Fletcher	Graeme / Elvis / Hospital Security Guard
Con O'Neill	Vince
Samantha Robinson	Cindy
Jess Schofield	Kelly / Vicki / Nurse
Alan Stocks	Frank

Thanks to extras from Dolphin Dance studios, Liverpool John Moores University, Liverpool Community College, Liverpool Theatre College, Liverpool School of English, Riverside Drama Department, TrEAD and our kind volunteers.

Company

Writer	**Robert Farquhar**
Director	**Matt Wilde**
Set, Costume and Video Design	**Simon Daw**
Lighting Designer	**Paul Anderson**
Sound Designer	**Tom Gibbons**
Choreographer	**Aline David**
Costume Supervisor	**Jacquie Davies**
Casting Director (*Dead Heavy Fantastic,* *'Tis Pity She's a Whore* and *Anthology*)	**Kay Magson CDG**
Assistant Director	**John Ward**
Production Manager	**Sean Pritchard**
Company Manager	**Paul Sawtell**
Stage Manager	**Sarah Lewis**
Deputy Stage Manager	**Roxanne Vella**
Assistant Stage Manager	**Kate Foster**
Lighting Operator	**Andy Webster**
Sound and AV Operator	**Ian Davies**
Stage Crew	**Xenia Bayer, Lindsey Bell, Howard Macaulay**
Wardrobe Mistress	**Brenna Mackenzie**
Video Programmer	**Jack James**
Assistant Cameraman	**Joshua Sessions**
Set Built By	**Splinter**
Production Photographer	**Helen Warner**

For this production, the Company wishes to thank: Silverberg Opticians; the Liverpool Film Office; the Everyman Youth Theatre; Clarks the Butchers; Mark Woods, Enterprise Liverpool Council; Leanne Wilson, Helen Kirkham and the security at The Royal Liverpool University Hospital; The Casa; John Hopwood, Liverpool City Council; Steven Hesketh and Jennifer Hughes of Bridge Street Apartments, Liverpool One; Frank Baker, Liverpool One; The bar at FACT and Alma de Cuba.

Cast (in alphabetical order)

Michelle Butterly
Maureen

Theatre credits include:
Naughts and Crosses (RSC and tour); Ma Vie En Rose (Young Vic); I Like Mine With a Kiss (Bush Theatre); Speaking Like Magpies, A New Way To Please You, Believe What You Will and Thomas More (RSC / Stratford and Trafalgar Studios); Gone to Earth (Shared Experience / Tour); The People Are Friendly (Royal Court); A Servant to Two Masters (RSC and West End); Road and Shakers (Wolsey Theatre, Ipswich); End of the Food Chain (Stephen Joseph Theatre); Laundry Room at the Hotel Madrid (Gate Theatre, London); Lent (Belgrade Studio, Coventry) and Gaslight (Theatr Clwyd).

Television credits include:
Beautiful People (Series 1 and 2), Midsomer Murders, Doctors, Minder, No Angels (Series 2); Eyes Down, Dangerfield, Pie in the Sky, Hetty Wainthrop Investigates, Soldier Soldier, St Clare, The Echo, Heartbeat and Casualty.

Film credits include:
Chromophobia.

Radio credits include:
Death of a Pirate.

David Carlyle
Stevie / Preacher / Young Man at Karaoke

David graduated from Rose Bruford in July 2010.

Since graduating his theatre credits include:
Caledonia (National Theatre of Scotland / EIF) and David Greig's newest play The Monster in the Hall (TAG / Citizens Theatre).

Credits whilst training include:
Anthony Neilson's The Wonderful World of Dissocia, Philistines, The White Devil, Ibsen's Hedda Gabler and Harold Pinter's Celebration and Party Time.

Prior to training at Rose Bruford, David also studied for one year at LIPA credits there include Nicholas Nickleby and The Country Wife.

David also represented Rose Bruford in the 2010 Sam Wanamaker Festival at Shakespeare's Globe Theatre playing Flamenio in The White Devil.

Radio credits include:
Sudbary Hill for Theatre503.

David is delighted to be coming back to Liverpool and working at the Everyman Theatre.

Helen Carter
Julie / Dee / Goldfish Woman / Dawn

Liverpool born Helen trained at LAMDA.

Theatre credits include:
No Wise Men; *Once Upon a Time at the Adelphi* which won Best Musical Production at the 2008 TMA Theatre Awards and *The Flint Street Nativity* (Liverpool Playhouse); *Hatch* (24:7 Theatre Festival and Bolton Octagon); *Dad's Army Marches On* (No. 1 Tour); *Slappers and Slapheads* (Royal Court, Liverpool); *Top Girls (London Royal Court)* and *The Honest Whore* (Globe Theatre, William Poetry Festival).

Television credits include:
Doctors, Judge John Deed, Beaten and *A470*.

Stephen Fletcher
Graeme / Elvis / Hospital Security Guard

Stephen trained at LIPA.

Theatre credits include:
Scouse Pacific, Lennon, Our Day Out and *Stags and Hens – 30th Anniversary Remix* (Royal Court, Liverpool); *57 Hours in The House of Culture* (Workshop) (The National Theatre Studio); *Up on the Roof* (Oldham Coliseum / The New Wolsey); *Hamlet, Rosencrantz* and *Guildenstern are Dead* and *A Midsummer Night's Dream* (Liverpool Shakespeare Festival); *Cinderella* (Liverpool Empire); *Eric's* (Liverpool Everyman); *Mary Stuart* (The Donmar and West End); *The Safari Party* (The New Vic); *Comfort* (Old Vic); *7 Stories* (Etcetera); *100% Bullet Proof* (Soho Theatre); John Godber's *Teechers* (Dubai); Willy Russell's *Breezeblock Park* (Liverpool Playhouse); *Betwixt: The Musical* (The King's Head); *Top of the Heap / Cassanova Returns* (Cardiff Global Search for a new musical Festival); *The Wild Party* (Edinburgh Fringe); *She Loves Me* and *Follies (LIPA)* and *Falsettoland (N.S.T.C / Edinburgh festival)*.

Television credits include:
Emmerdale, The Liverpool Nativity, BRITZ, All About Me, Kerching, Ricky's Joke Shop and *Heartbeat*.

Cast (in alphabetical order)

Con O'Neill
Vince

Theatre credits include:
Salome (UK Tour); *Faces in the Crowd*
(Royal Court); *The Female of the Species*
(Vaudeville); *The Caretaker* (Sheffield
Theatre / Tricycle Theatre); *Midnight
Cowboy* (Assembly Theatre Edinburgh);
Southwark Fair and *Blasted* (National
Theatre); *Telestar* (No 1 Tour / West End
– nominated for an Oliver award); *Mother
Claps Molly House* (National Theatre /
Aldwych); *Featuring Loretta, The Flight Into
Egypt, The Fastest Clock in the Universe*
and *The Awakening* (Hampstead Theatre);
A Tribute to the Blues Brothers (Whitehall
Theatre – wrote / co-produced, nominated
for an Olivier award); *Woyzeck* (Hull Truck
Theatre) and *Blood Brothers* (West End
/ Broadway – winner of an Oliver Award,
nominated for a Tony Award).

Television credits include:
*Margot, Criminal Justice, Learners,
The Stepfather, Ultimate Force, The
Illustrated Mum, In Deep, Trail and
Retribution VI, Waking the Dead, Real
Women II, Always and Everyone, Cider with
Rosie, Heartbeat, Macbeth, Tom Jones,
Wycliffe, Peak Practise, Soldier Soldier,
Moving Story; Inspector Morse, Casualty,
Pie in the Sky, The Riff Raff Element,
Amongst Barbarians, One Summer* and
Norbert Smith.

Film credits include:
*Frank, The Kid, Telstar, What's Your Name
41, The Last Seduction II, Bedrooms and
Hallways, A Perfect Match, Three Steps To
Heaven, Scarborough Ahoy! The Lilac Bus*
and *Dancin' Thru The Dark.*

Samantha Robinson
Cindy

Samantha trained at Rose Bruford.

Theatre credits include:
Hansel and Gretel (Core, Northampton);
The House of Bernarda Alba (Nuffield Theatre);
Proper Clever (Liverpool Playhouse); *Three
Sisters on Hope Street* (Liverpool Everyman
and Hampstead Theatre); *The Tempest*
(Royal Exchange); *The Three Musketeers*
(Bristol Old Vic); *A Taste of Honey* (Oldham
Coliseum Theatre and Tour); *The Laramie
Project* (Sound Theatre, Leicester Square);
The Lemon Princess (West Yorkshire
Playhouse); *The Owl Service* (Plymouth
Theatre Royal); *Untouchable* (The Bush
Theatre) and *Song of the Western Men*
(Chichester Festival Theatre).

Television credits include:
*Five Days, Casualty, Doctors, Holby City,
Shameless, The Girl Who Came To Stay*
and *Island at War.*

Film credits include:
Sixty Six and *Jamaica Me Crazy.*

Radio credits include:
Several for BBC Radio 4 including
The Believers, Life with Lisa and
Evaristo's Epitaph.

Jess Schofield
Kelly / Vicki / Nurse

Jess was born in Liverpool and trained at the Liverpool Theatre School. She was a member of the Everyman Youth Theatre from the age of thirteen.

Theatre credits include:
The Vagina Monologues and *Lost Soul (Royal Court, Liverpool).*

Television credits include:
Justice and *Moving On.*

Radio credits include:
Nige's Day Out and *The Last Ferry Home.*

Alan Stocks
Frank

Theatre credits include:
Scouse Pacific, Night Collar, Ladies Night, A Fistful of Collars, Funny Money and *Slappers and Slapheads* (Royal Court, Liverpool); *Dirty Dusting* (Liverpool Empire); *Tartuffe* and *The Flint Street Nativity* (Liverpool Playhouse); *Twelfth Night* (Lyric Belfast); *Measure for Measure, The Two Gentlemen of Verona* and *the Merchant of Venice* (RSC); *The Starving* (Pointsfield Theatre); *Nervous Breakdown* (Warehouse Theatre); *End of the Food Chain* (Stephen Joseph Theatre) and *Sleeping Beauty, Love at a Loss, 'Tis Pity She's a Whore, Wild Wild Women* and *Trojan Women* (Liverpool Everyman).

Television credits include:
Phone Shop, Casualty 1907, Kingdom, Robin Hood, Ghostboat, Doctors, Blue Blood, Wire in the Blood, The Plan Man, Rome, Merseybeat, This Little Life, Casualty, Auf Wiedersehen Pet, Combat Sheep, Kingdom, City Central, Dad, Drop the Dead Donkey, Murder in Mind, Eastenders, North Square, Stalkers, Sins, Dockers, This Life, Wycliffe, Grushko, The Day Today, Soldier Soldier, Conviction, Between the Lines, Sweet Nothing and *You Me and Him.*

Film credits include:
Memory of Water, Shadowman, Green Fingers, The Birthday Girl, Under Suspicion Trigger Puller, The Pond and *Look At Me I'm Beautiful.*

Radio credits include:
Tartuffe.

Company

Robert Farquhar
Writer

Plays include:
You Are Here, The Angry Kitchen Sink, Empty the Thought-Bubble, Almost Forever But, Kissing Sid James, Gods Official, Dust to Dust, and *Bad Jazz.* The last four of these have been published by Josef Weinberger. They have mostly received their first performances at the Unity Theatre, but have since been performed in theatres around the UK, including Liverpool Everyman, West Yorkshire Playhouse, Hull Truck, Edinburgh Traverse, Bolton Octagon, Stephen Joseph Scarborough, Oldham Coliseum and Plymouth Drum. They have also been performed internationally in countries such as the United States, Italy, Canada, Australia, Ireland, Malta, and Slovakia. Also *Eddie Kavanagh's Jacket* (Everyman 40th anniversary gala); *When I Wake Up I Want to Be Famous* (Fuse Theatre); *A Word Doesn't Exist* (Slung Low / Liverpool Everyman *Anthology)* and *Something To Believe In* (Lime Pictures / Channel Four).

He is a member of Big Wow Theatre Company, and scripts and directs all their shows, including *Swanky Geezer Nonsense, Dark Grumblings, Insomnobabble,* and *The Friendship Experiment.* They have recently been commissioned by BBC Radio Four to develop *Insomnobabble* into a four-part series.

Matt Wilde
Director

Matt Wilde is a former Associate Director of the NT Studio and Out of Joint.

Recent work in Liverpool includes:
Lost Monsters by Laurence Wilson (Liverpool Everyman); *On Tour* by Gregory Burke (Royal Court London and Liverpool Everyman) and *One Night In Istanbul* by Nicky Allt (Liverpool Empire).

Other work includes:
Splendour by Abi Morgan (GBS Theatre, RADA); *Out of Focus* by Gabriel Bissett-Smith / Shireen Mula / Tash Rickman (Only Connect Theatre, London); *The Wonderful World of Dissocia* by Anthony Neilson (Unicorn Theatre, London); *Nocturne* by Adam Rapp (Almeida Theatre); *Branded* by Simon Bent (Old Vic); *Stoning Mary* by Debbie Tucker Green (Teatro Flumen. Valencia); *Get Tested* by Laura Wade and *The Elephant In The Room* by Laurence Marks and Maurice Gran (Celebrity 24hr Plays at Old Vic); *Out of the Fog* by Roy Williams (Almeida Theatre); *Polar Bear* by Mark Schultz (Birmingham Rep / ATC); *On The Middle Day* by Gavin Birch (Old Vic @ IWM) and *Gizmo Love* by John Kolvenbach (ATC). For the National Theatre he directed *Slow Time* by Roy Williams, co-directed the *His Dark Materials* Revival by Nicholas Wright and was Associate Director on *Stuff Happens* by David Hare and *Jumpers* by Tom Stoppard.

Matt is involved in developing and producing new work with writers from the Royal Court London, Old Vic New Voices, British Council, Soho Theatre, Liverpool Everyman, NT Studio, Goldsmith's College, Rose Bruford College and RADA.

Simon Daw
Set, Costume and Video Design

Recent stage design credits include:
As One (Royal Ballet); Romeo and Juliet (Shakespeare's Globe); Double Sentence (Soho Theatre); Lost Monsters (Liverpool Everyman); Dolls (National Theatre Scotland); Fast Labour (Hampstead Theatre / West Yorkshire Playhouse); DNA, Baby Girl, The Miracle and The Enchantment (National Theatre); Elling (Bush and Trafalgar Studios); French Without Tears (English Touring Theatre); Rutherford and Son, Rafts and Dreams and Across Oka (Royal Exchange, Manchester); Romeo and Juliet (RSC, Stratford / Albery); Adam and Eve (TPT, Tokyo); Kebab (Royal Court Theatre Upstairs); Bloom (Rambert) and The Stepfather (Candoco).

Installation / performance commissions include:
3rd Ring Out (UK tour); Wavestructures, Hopefully it Means Nothing and Sea House (Aldeburgh Festival) and New Town (site specific / Arches).

Paul Anderson
Lighting Designer

Paul Anderson trained at Mountview Theatre School and York College of Arts and Technology.

Lighting designs include:
A Dog's Heart (DNO/ENO); Blood and Gifts, Nation, The Revengers Tragedy, A Minute Too Late, Stuff Happens, A Funny Thing Happened on the Way to the Forum, Measure for Measure, Cyrano de Bergerac and The Birds (National Theatre); Shirley Valentine, Educating Rita, Endgame, Arcadia, Treasure Island, Swimming with Sharks, Little Shop of Horrors, Underneath the Lintel, The Tempest, On The Third Day, Someone Who'll Watch Over Me, Simply Heavenly, A Servant to Two Masters and Lenny Henry's So Much Things to Say (All West End); All My Sons, The Chairs (nominated for Tony, Drama Desk and Olivier awards); The Resistible Rise of Arturo Ui (National Actors Theatre New York with Al Pacino); Julius Caesar, The Tempest and A Servant to Two Masters (Royal Shakespeare Company); Shun-kin, A Disappearing Number, Strange Poetry, The Elephant Vanishes, Light, The Noise of Time and Mnemonic (Drama Desk and Lucille Lortell award), (Theatre de Complicite); On Tour and Random and Incomplete Acts of Kindness (Royal Court); Singer, Americans and The Inland Sea (Oxford Stage Company); Two Cities, Playing for Time and Taming of the Shrew (Salisbury Playhouse); 20,000 Leagues Under the Sea and Shoot to Win (Theatre Royal Stratford East) and The Enchanted Pig, Simply Heavenly, Arabian Nights, As I lay Dying and Twelfth Night (Young Vic Theatre).

Company

Tom Gibbons
Sound Designer

Tom trained at Central School of
Speech and Drama in Theatre Sound
and is resident sound designer for the
international physical theatre company
Parrot{in the}Tank.

Recent design credits include:
Plenty (Crucible Studio, Sheffield); *Love,
Love, Love* (Paines Plough, National Tour);
The Chairs (Ustinov Bath); *The Country,
The Road To Mecca, The Roman Bath,
1936* and *The Shawl* (Arcola); *The
Knowledge, Little Platoons, 50 Ways To
Leave Your Lover, 50 Ways To Leave Your
Lover@Xmas* and *Broken Space Season*
(Bush Theatre); *Bagpuss, Everything
Must Go* and *Soho Streets* (Soho Theatre);
The Machine Gunners (Polka); *Holes*
(New Wimbledon Studio); *Terror Tales*
(Hampstead Studio); *The Hostage* and
Present Tense (Southwark Playhouse);
Faustus (Watford Palace, Tour); *Faithless
Bitches* (Courtyard); *FAT* (The Oval House,
National Tour); *Just Me Bell* (Graeae, Tour);
Blue Heaven (Finborough); *Pitching In*
(Latitude Festival, Tour); *US Love Bites*
(Old Red Lion, Tristan Bates); *I Can Sing
A Rainbow* with Nabocov and Sheffield
Theatres (Lyceum Sheffield); *Pendulum*
(Jermyn Street); *Journalist and Hope*
(ICA London); *Machinal* (Central) and *Bar
Of Ideas* (Paradise Gardens Festival and
Glastonbury / Shangri-La).

As Associate Designer:
The Aliens (Bush Theatre).

Aline David
Choreographer

Choreography includes:
Greenland and Our Class (National Theatre);
Wanderlust (Royal Court); *How to Be an
Other Woman* (The Gate); *Alice* (Sheffield
Crucible); *Eurydice* (with ATC) and *Elektra*
(Young Vic); *1984* and *Macbeth* (Royal
Exchange Manchester); *A Christmas Carol*
(The Sherman Theatre, Cardiff); *Troilus* and
Cressida (Shakespeare's Globe); *Tarantula*
(Petrol Blue at Aldeburgh, Snape Maltings
Concert Hall); *The Brothers Size* (Young Vic
and on tour) and *Gone Too Far!* (Royal Court /
Actors Touring Company – Winner of 2008
Laurence Olivier Award for Outstanding
Achievement in an Affiliated Theatre).

As a performer:
Swan Lake (Ballet du Rhin); *Cendrillon,
La Grande Duchesse, L'Italiana in Algeria*
and *L'Africaine* (Rhin National Opera);
The Tempest (Rhin National Opera, the
ROH and Royal Opera House Copenhagen);
Le Barbier de Seville (Palais des Congres
et de la Musique de Strasbourg) and
The Queen of Spades (the ROH).

Jacquie Davies
Costume Supervisor

Theatre credits include:
Sleeping Beauty, 'Tis Pity She's a Whore, Anthology, The Ragged Trousered Philanthropists, Dick Whittington, The Caretaker, Lost Monsters, Billy Wonderful, Mother Goose, Endgame, Eric's, Intemperance, The Way Home, The Morris and *Port Authority* (Liverpool Everyman); *Oedipus, Canary, Ghost Stories, The Hypochondriac, The Price, Our Country's Good, Tartuffe* and *Once Upon a Time at the Adelphi* (Liverpool Playhouse); *Vurt, Wise Guys, Unsuitable Girls* and *Perfect* (Contact Theatre, Manchester); *Oleanna* and *Memory* (Clwyd Theatr Cymru); *Love on the Dole* (The Lowry, Manchester); *Never the Sinner* (Library Theatre, Manchester) and *Shockheaded Peter* (West End).

Opera credits include work at:
Scottish Opera, Buxton Opera Festival, Music Theatre Wales and *Opera Holland Park.*

Television and film credits include:
Queer As Folk, The Parole Officer, I Love the 1970s and *1980s, Brookside* and *Hollyoaks.*

Design credits include:
Kes, Saturday, Sunday, Monday, Oh What a Lovely War, Into the Woods, The Rover, Titus Andronicus, Pericles, Spring Awakening, Twelfth Night, Macbeth, The Red Balloon, The Weirdstone of Brisingamen, Perfect, The Cherry Orchard, Machinal and *Trelawny of the Wells.*

Kay Magson CDG
Casting Director

Theatre credits include:
'Tis Pity She's a Whore and *Anthology* (Liverpool Everyman / Slung Low); *The Solid Gold Cadillac* (Garrick); *Dangerous Corner* (West Yorkshire Playhouse / West End); *Round the Horne… Revisited* and *Dracula* (National Tours); *Singin' in the Rain* (West Yorkshire Playhouse, NT / National tour); *Aspects of Love, All The Fun of the Fair* and *The Witches of Eastwick* (National Tours); *Kes* (Liverpool Playhouse and National Tour); *Great Expectations* (ETT / Watford and National Tour) and *Sweeney Todd* (Royal Festival Hall).

Kay was resident at the West Yorkshire Playhouse for 17 years where she cast many shows including *Hamlet, The McKellen Ensemble Season, The Patrick Stewart Priestley Season* and many others, and also casts regularly for Salisbury Playhouse, Northampton Theatres (including *Young America* at the NT), Hull Truck and the Manchester Library Theatre.

She has just completed casting on *Walk Like a Panther,* a pilot TV for Finite Films.

Kay is a member of the Casting Director's Guild of Great Britain (CDG).

Company

John Ward
Assistant Director

Assistant director credits include:
Carmen (Leicester Square Theatre); *A Street Car Named Desire* (Nuffield Theatre); *Henry V* (Chichester Festival Theatre) and *The Misanthrope* (Theatre Royal Drum).

Directing credits include:
A Perfect Circle (Zoo venues Edinburgh); *Our Country's Good* (on tour); *The Perfect Girl* (Old Red Lion) and has directed various productions for drama schools.

John is Artistic director of DumbWise, for which he has developed and directed a number of new plays.

John trained as a director at Rose Bruford College.

Liverpool Everyman and Playhouse staff

DEAD HEAVY FANTASTIC

DEAD HEAVY FANTASTIC

by Robert Farquhar

JOSEF WEINBERGER PLAYS

LONDON

DEAD HEAVY FANTASTIC
First published in 2011
by Josef Weinberger Ltd
12-14 Mortimer Street, London, W1T 3JJ
www.josef-weinberger.com
plays@jwmail.co.uk

ISBN 978 085676 318 2

Printed in England by Commercial Colour Press plc, Hainault, Essex

For Sue. She's always done it her way.

"Why am I here?
I'm here because I've got no fucking choice"
Me White Noise – Blur

With special thanks and gratitude to
Suzanne Bell, Gemma Bodinetz, Phil Breen, Matt
Wilde, Eddy Marshall, Charlotte Knight, Matt
Rutter and Tim Lynsky.

CHARACTERS

FRANK

CINDY

VINCE

GRAEME

MAUREEN

JULIE

KELLY

STEVIE

DEE

VICKY

DAWN

PREACHER

NURSE

YOUNG MAN AT KARAOKE, WOMAN WITH GOLDFISH,
SECURITY GUARD, ELVIS

Scene One

A deep throb of music. Builds.

A series of fast cut images. Dancing. Lights. Nightlife. A message flashed up within it:

HAVE A GOOD TIME ALL THE TIME

Music and film cut out.

A trendy drinking establishment. FRANK, *late thirties, could be older, sits alone. Obviously waiting for someone.*

CINDY *enters. A glam edge to her, in direct contrast to* FRANK. *Gathers herself. She approaches* FRANK.

CINDY   Excuse me, are you . . .

             (FRANK *turns.*)

CINDY   Are you Frank?

             (FRANK *doesn't answer straightaway.*)

FRANK   Right, of course. I'm, er, yea, I'm, I'm Frank.

CINDY   I'm Cindy.

FRANK   Right. Well, that's lucky.

CINDY   Why's that?

FRANK   You know, because, I, well, I'm supposed to be
             meeting someone called Cindy.

CINDY   That's me.

FRANK   I know I was just, er . . .

             (CINDY *realises lame attempt at joke.*)

CINDY   Oh. Sorry. I thought –

FRANK No, no. No.

CINDY You were saying you thought I was someone else.

FRANK I'm just saying stuff –

CINDY Because –

FRANK Don't listen to me –

CINDY I thought you were probably thinking I wasn't going to show up.

FRANK No.

CINDY Were you thinking that?

FRANK No. Honestly, I –

CINDY I bet you were.

FRANK I wasn't.

CINDY Not that I know what goes on inside other people's heads. Because I'm not psychic or anything like that.

FRANK Seriously, I –

CINDY Sorry, that probably sounded a bit weird.

FRANK I didn't think anything like that.

(*A slight moment.*)

CINDY Do you think I could have a drink Frank?

FRANK Now that. Good idea. What would you like?

CINDY (*immediately*) Vodka.

FRANK What? Just straightforward . . .

CINDY Yea.

FRANK   Vodka?

CINDY   A double.

FRANK   Right. Okay. Yes. I will, you, er, you just stay
there, and I will, yea, sort that out. On my way.

*(FRANK exits, all nervous energy. CINDY sits,
thinking. A muffled mobile ringing. It is coming
from her handbag.)*

CINDY   *(to herself)* Go on then. Yea. I'm not answering it.
Do you hear me?

(It carries on ringing.)

CINDY   Do you hear me? I said . . .

*(She relents, and pulls it out of the handbag. She
answers it.)*

CINDY   I'm not answering it alright.

*(She cuts the caller off. FRANK returns with
drinks.)*

FRANK   Right then. Here we go.

CINDY   Oh, ta very much Frank.

FRANK   One vodka, large. And one lager. Pint.

(Then fetches out.)

FRANK   And one packet of nuts, posh. You know, just in
case . . .

CINDY   Frank?

FRANK   What?

(She weighs up the moment.)

CINDY   Your picture on the website. I really liked it.

FRANK   Right. Thanks very much.

CINDY   Because I bet a lot of people, I bet they cheat.

FRANK   Do you think?

CINDY   And I just thought, you know, you had a really, really nice face.

FRANK   Well, that's very . . .

CINDY   A bit like my Dad.

FRANK   Oh . . .

CINDY   I don't mean, not like he is now. When he was forty-odd.

FRANK   Okay.

CINDY   Because he's –

FRANK   Even though I'm only thirty-nine.

CINDY   He's sixty something now, and got a hearing aid.

FRANK   Has he?

CINDY   Because my Mum threw him out. You know, because she said he was always ignoring her, but really it was because he was going deaf.

FRANK   Right.

CINDY   And then when I saw your picture, I thought, it reminded me of, like my Dad. You know, dead normal, and uncomplicated.

FRANK   Well, I suppose –

(CINDY *suddenly decides to leave.*)

CINDY   Look. I'm really, I'm sorry Frank, but –

FRANK   Hey. Whoa. What are you doing?

CINDY   I'm going go, get off. Because –

FRANK   Eh? No.

CINDY   I'm not really sure why I'm here. And it's not because I don't like you Frank, because I do . . .

FRANK   Don't go then.

CINDY   But I don't know what I'm doing.

FRANK   Well, stay then. Have another drink. You've only just got here.

(CINDY *doesn't leave.*)

FRANK   And I know, something like this, it's, all a bit, you know, venturing into the unknown and that, and tonight, well, it has all been very last minute, but I don't think, you know, and I'm not just saying this, because, but, well, you seem, very nice, and, we're here now aren't we, eh? And, to be honest, I'm not that au fait with, with what you're supposed to do when you meet up with, someone like this. Although, the other week, someone did get in touch. And, we, yea, we, er, and I did, maybe, talk about my wife, ex-wife, a bit too much. But I'm not, we are divorced, paperwork all signed off. And now you're probably thinking I'm not really, you know, but no, won't mention it again. Not the case. No. I'm just thinking about the future now.

(FRANK *has made a speech.*)

FRANK   We can just be two people having a drink. That's all. However you want to play it.

CINDY   That was lovely Frank.

FRANK   Well, it does seem a bit of a shame, if you –

CINDY   Do you want to go on somewhere else?

FRANK   Er, yea. That sounds . . .

CINDY   It's not far.

FRANK   Okay. Yea.

CINDY   Let's go now.

FRANK   Why not?

CINDY   Because it's only just round the corner, and –

FRANK   Yea, let's go for it.

CINDY   I've got some condoms.

FRANK   Let me just. Whoa. Hold on.

CINDY   Come on Frank. It's only about two, three minutes.

FRANK   No, Cindy. No. Can I –

CINDY   Leave that.

FRANK   Whoa, whoa. Hold on. Can we just –

CINDY   Leave it. Let's go. Now. Come on.

FRANK   No. Stop. Stop. Stop!

                (*They look at each other.*)

FRANK   Did you just say –

CINDY   I like you Frank.

FRANK   Well, I appreciate that, but –

CINDY   And if you like somebody –

FRANK   Yea, but Cindy . . .

CINDY   Why not just say so?

FRANK   Yea, but, fucking hell, it's, sorry, sorry, I didn't
            mean to say that.

CINDY   Say what?

FRANK   Before when I was on my way out tonight, I made
            a bit of a promise to myself, no swearing, because –

CINDY   That's alright, Frank.

FRANK   You want to make a good impression don't you?

CINDY   I don't mind if you want to swear.

FRANK   Okay, ta. But can I, what if right, what, what if

CINDY   What if what Frank?

FRANK   What if I was some sort of weirdo, or –

CINDY   Are you a weirdo?

FRANK   No.

CINDY   Well, that's alright then.

FRANK   No. I didn't mean that. I meant –

CINDY   Come on.

FRANK   Can't we, say, go to the pictures, or –

CINDY   Go to the pictures?

FRANK   And I don't want you to think, because. That's
            not what I'm saying.

CINDY   Do you not want to have sex with me Frank?

FRANK   No, that's what I'm saying. I'm not saying that.

CINDY   I've just asked you to make love to me.

FRANK   I know, make love? You said have sex a minute
             ago?

CINDY   What's the difference?

FRANK   I don't know. That's what I'm asking.

             (CINDY *walks over, and kisses* FRANK. *She steps
             back.*)

CINDY   What do you want to do Frank?

             (*They look at each other.*)

FRANK   After you.

             (*As they turn to exit, the stage explodes with the
             beginnings of city night life. Lights. Noise. A hen
             party.* KELLY, JULIE, *and* MAUREEN, *all dressed
             appropriately. They flirt with a passing man. He
             enjoys it. In the midst of all this, appears a street
             preacher speaking through a small PA system.*)

PREACHER   And let me just say this, because there will come a
             day when you will be judged. You will stand
             before God, and he will ask you what you did with
             your life. Because do not be swayed from the
             correct and true pathway. Because we live in an
             era of moral decay. Where people smoke too much,
             drink too much, have casual sexual relations too
             much. And the Bible tells us we do these things to
             suppress our real selves. Because man is not an
             animal. Do you hear this? Man is not an animal.

             (*A voice from somewhere, 'Knobhead'.*)

                          Scene Two

A small bedroom in a hotel somewhere nearby. CINDY *and*
FRANK *fall into the room.*

CINDY   Okay Frank. Here we are.

FRANK   Yea. Right. It's, yea, it's, yea.

CINDY   Have a drink.

             (CINDY *has produced a small bottle of something
             from her handbag. Swigs it, and passes to* FRANK.
             Takes out her mobile.)

FRANK   Okay. Yea. I'll have a drink.

             (CINDY *takes out her mobile and starts to text
             something.*)

CINDY   Enjoying yourself Frank?

FRANK   Oh yea. This is, yea, I'm very, absolutely, er –

CINDY   My Nan has that picture . . .

FRANK   Oh right. Very nice.

CINDY   I always thought it was really horrible.

FRANK   Yea, well, it's not what you'd call great art is it.

CINDY   I'm just going go in here . . .

FRANK   Okay. You do that.

CINDY   I won't be long.

FRANK   Sure thing. You, yea, you, fine by me.

             (*She exits into bathroom. With mobile. She shouts
             through.*)

CINDY   What are you doing Frank?

FRANK   Er, not a lot. Just, hanging about.

CINDY   What's the bed like?

FRANK   You what?

CINDY   The bed? What's it like?

FRANK   Er. Yea. It . . . seems alright.

CINDY   Not too bouncy?

FRANK   No. It's, no. It's –

             (FRANK *is now trying out the bed.*)

CINDY   Or too hard?

FRANK   I don't think so. I mean, there is, you know, there
             is a bit of give, but –

             (CINDY *emerges from bathroom.*)

CINDY   What you saying Frank?

FRANK   I was saying, the, er. Actually it's quite comfy.

CINDY   Quite comfy?

FRANK   Yea.

             (*Sexual tension.* CINDY *starts to unbutton
             something. Goes on for some time.*)

FRANK   Look, shall we . . .

CINDY   What are you doing?

FRANK   I was going do something to the lighting.

CINDY   No Frank.

FRANK   I know some people prefer it if –

CINDY   We don't need to do anything to the lighting
             Frank.

(FRANK *leaves the lighting. Sits back down.*)

CINDY   Sorry, it's just, I –

FRANK   Not a problem. If that's what you like.

CINDY   What's your favourite position?

            (FRANK *doesn't answer straightaway.*)

CINDY   Everybody has a favourite position.

FRANK   Oh. Right. You mean –

            (FRANK *laughs slightly.*)

CINDY   Why are you laughing Frank?

FRANK   No, it's alright. It's just, for a moment there, I
            thought you were talking about football.

CINDY   What?

FRANK   It's just when you said –

CINDY   Why would I be talking about football?

FRANK   I know. That's what I'm saying. I thought, but
            then I, I don't know why I said that. Sorry.

            (*A moment, and then* CINDY *makes a move. They
            kiss, and fall back on the bed.* FRANK *pulls
            something.*)

FRANK   Ow. Bugger.

CINDY   What is it?

FRANK   It's alright, it was just, when I was leaning back –

CINDY   Let's get these trousers off . . .

FRANK   Right, okay, yea, just, watch the zip. It can be a bit
            temperamental.

(As FRANK *proceeds to undo his trousers, a man sidles into the room. This is* VINCE. *He observes.* CINDY *starts to perform a little bit more.)*

CINDY   Come on Frank. Let's see what's down there.

FRANK   Okay. Just. Let me get myself a bit more.

CINDY   I want you to fuck me good and hard Frank.

FRANK   Okay. Yea. That sounds, er, just, if I could just –

CINDY   What are you doing?

FRANK   I just want to get my shoes off.

CINDY   Look –

FRANK   It'll be easier in the long run.

CINDY   Frank . . .

FRANK   I know it seems a bit of a faff, but –

               *(*FRANK *leans forward, and tumbles off the bed. Trousers now round his ankles.)*

CINDY   Oh Frank, for, will you please. I want you in me Frank. Now.

FRANK   I'm sorry Cindy. I know you said –

CINDY   What are you doing?

               *(*FRANK *has got to his feet, and is heading towards the light switch.)*

FRANK   It's just I'd feel happier, if –

CINDY   Frank!

FRANK   It was just a bit more conducive, lighting-wise.

(FRANK *turns down the lights. A moment. Then brings them back up. He has seen* VINCE.)

FRANK Who, eh, eh, who –

VINCE I'm just passing through, mate.

FRANK Who the flaming hell is that?

VINCE You carry on. Go for it.

CINDY Yea. Ignore him, Frank.

FRANK Eh? Are you, oh right. Okay. I see.

  (FRANK *starts to try and pull his trousers back up.*)

CINDY Come on Frank.

FRANK No. This is, really, I am not into anything like this.

VINCE Hey. Do you see what he's thinking? Eh?

CINDY Will you just go away Vince?

VINCE Oh, what, you, eh, you're fucking unbelievable you.

FRANK I don't know what's going on here, but –

  (FRANK *tries to push his way past.*)

VINCE Frank. Seriously, fill your socks.

CINDY Leave him alone!

VINCE Have a party mate. Go on.

FRANK Can I just –

CINDY Stop that Vince. Will you, leave off him.

  (CINDY *shoves* VINCE.)

VINCE   Alright, fuck it, if that's what you want.

FRANK   Excuse me –

VINCE   I'll leave you and your sad, loser, beastie boy, big
             bollocks boyfriend here –

CINDY   Don't say that Vince, because –

FRANK   I want to get past . . .

CINDY   Frank is not some sad loser.

VINCE   Is he not, eh? Because he – Frank – Will you stop
             that? Because he looks like one.

FRANK   I want to leave. Can you –

VINCE   You're staying, mate.

FRANK   Just get out of the way.

             (FRANK *attempts a little bit more force to try and
             extricate himself from the room. This only
             escalates the situation.*)

VINCE   Crying out loud Frank.

FRANK   I want to leave.

VINCE   You're staying here.

             (VINCE *reacts to* FRANK'S *efforts to leave the room.
             Grabs* FRANK, *and holds him in a strange,
             demeaning sort of headlock. A certain amount of
             chaos now breaks out.*)

CINDY   No Vince. Stop it. Stop it.

             (*Ad lib verbiage if necessary.*)

VINCE   Oh you want to have a go do you Frank? Eh?
             Fancy a little bit of shove about do you?

FRANK   Get off. Ow.

CINDY   Leave him alone Vince!

FRANK   You're hurting my ears!

CINDY   You're hurting his ears!

VINCE   How's that Frank? How's that eh? Is that alright
            for you is it?

CINDY   Vince! Will you, just, let him go! Now.

            (VINCE *releases* FRANK *from his headlock.*)

VINCE   Alright. There we go. Frank is let go. Everyone
            happy? Eh?

            (FRANK *launches a punch in* VINCE'S *direction.*
            VINCE *dodges it, but reacts by throwing one back.*
            FRANK *is winded and falls to the floor.*)

CINDY   Jesus Christ, Vince. What did you do that for?

VINCE   He had a swing. You saw him!

CINDY   Frank? Are you okay? Can you hear me?

VINCE   I mean, I'm not just going fucking stand here am I?

CINDY   How many fingers am I holding up?

VINCE   And I didn't even, I hardly. I partially winded him
            that's all.

CINDY   Just breathe normally.

VINCE   Do you hear me?

CINDY   Say something Frank.

VINCE   Oh bollocks to this, I'm going.

CINDY   Yea. Do one.

VINCE   Yea. Fuck you, you mad, fucking –

CINDY   Fuck you too Vince!

VINCE   Just fuck off!

CINDY   No you fuck off!

VINCE   Fuck off!!

             (VINCE *exits. A moment, and then he returns.*)

VINCE   Do you know what right? You, right, you. You do
             my head in you do.

             (*Exits. A moment, and then he returns.*)

VINCE   I'm a busy man. I don't need this.

             (*No response. He starts to exit, but then turns
             back.*)

VINCE   We need to talk.

             (VINCE *exits. Doesn't return this time.* CINDY
             reaches for her handbag.)

CINDY   Look Frank. Here's some aspirin. Don't take too
             many as you'll feel a bit weird. And they give you
             cancer.

             (*Hands him the aspirin.*)

CINDY   Or they stop you getting cancer. One of the two. I
             don't know. I read it somewhere.

             (*They look at each other.*)

CINDY   I'm really sorry Frank. It's, just, sometimes, I . . . I
             don't know what I'm doing.

             (*She exits.*)

Scene Three

Street outside. VINCE *leaving the hotel. As he does so the trio from the hen party from previous appear.* KELLY, JULIE, *and* MAUREEN. KELLY *is already steaming. She has just had an altercation with someone, off.*

KELLY   Oh eh, did you see the look on his face? He wasn't expecting that was he?

JULIE   You're off your head, you.

KELLY   (*shouting off*) Hey love. You're alright. I won't bite. Unless that's the sort of thing you're into.

JULIE   Don't say that. You'll give him nightmares!

KELLY   Eh come on, where are we? Where have they gone?

MAUREEN   I think they went in there.

KELLY   Right then. Let's find 'em.

               (*They cross over with* VINCE.)

KELLY   Hey you're sexy you aren't you. For an older bloke.

JULIE   Sorry mate, she doesn't get out much.

               (VINCE *doesn't really notice.* KELLY *disappears off into the bar. Singing a snatch of 'Its Raining Men'.* JULIE *notices that* MAUREEN *is lagging behind.*)

JULIE   Maureen? Are you alright?

MAUREEN   Yea. I'm fine. Really. I'm, just, er . . .

               (MAUREEN *is obviously considering getting off.*)

JULIE   Are you sure?

MAUREEN   Yea. I'm, honestly, I'm just . . .

JULIE   What?

            (*A* MAN *passes by.*)

MAN   Nice tits love.

JULIE   Ta for the feedback mate, but do us all a favour
            and go set fire to your head.

            (MAN *likes this response.*)

MAUREEN   Because, I do have to pick up the kids, I mean,
            really early tomorrow morning.

JULIE   Oh. Hey. No way.

MAUREEN   And I know that's my fault, because, I never learn
            do I, but, I've said it now haven't I, and I'm not
            sneaking off.

JULIE   No I know you're not. You're staying here.

MAUREEN   It's just . . .

JULIE   Maureen . . .

MAUREEN   I feel a bit of an idiot.

JULIE   Yea. And?

MAUREEN   Most of these girls. They're nearly half my age.

JULIE   No they're not.

MAUREEN   Well, I'm old enough to, you know, one or two of
            them, seriously, I could be their mother.

JULIE   I suppose that is about doable, but seeing as I
            know for a fact –

MAUREEN   I'm not exaggerating!

JULIE   You didn't have your first proper boyfriend until
             you were nineteen.

MAUREEN   Okay, so I was late starter, but that –

JULIE   Biologically, it's highly unlikely.

             (MAUREEN *takes this.*)

JULIE   Look. Come on. You deserve this.

MAUREEN   What? Why are you saying that?

JULIE   Because, you do. Because, and this is my serious
             face here, you haven't had it easy, have you?

MAUREEN   Yea, but –

JULIE   And you, Maureen, you are a very good looking,
             young –

MAUREEN   Don't be saying that!

JULIE   Young, middle-aged woman who –

MAUREEN   I knew that was too good to last!

JULIE   Well, you didn't let me finish did you?

MAUREEN   I am so sorry.

JULIE   Young, middle-aged woman, who –

MAUREEN   I think we all heard it the first time!

JULIE   Who needs to go out, have a laugh, and let her
             hair down.

             (*A moment is struck.* VINCE *re-enters.*)

JULIE   Is that understood? Maureen?

MAUREEN   Yes.

JULIE	Is that a proper yes?

MAUREEN   Yes. It's a proper yes. Yes. Understood. I, yes. I'm going have a laugh, and let my hair down.

JULIE   Well thank hallelujah for that. Now let's go and get shit-faced.

(They laugh, and start to move off.)

MAUREEN   But I'm not drinking any more of those blue things. They taste rank.

JULIE   And, hey, you never know, we might even get you a snog!

MAUREEN   Shut up!

JULIE   Because, look about girl, there's a lot of desperate men out there.

(They look at VINCE.*)*

MAUREEN   Cheeky cow.

(They exit. VINCE *is wondering what to do.* CINDY *stumbles from the hotel.)*

CINDY   *(to herself)* Right, do you know what, that's it. No way, am I –

(They see each other. A moment passes.)

VINCE   Cindy. Look –

CINDY   No Vince.

VINCE   Hey, come on. Don't be running off.

CINDY   Taxi!

VINCE   Let's sort this out.

(VINCE *touches her on the arm.*)

CINDY   Get off me Vince.

VINCE   Cindy?

CINDY   Will you just, get, leave me alone.

VINCE   Alright. Go on then. Are you, right, are you saying
            to me, you've seriously got a nose out of joint,
            because, and oh yea, thanks for the invite, by the
            way, because I just somehow turn up –

CINDY   I don't know what you're talking about.

VINCE   And walk in on some steamy, fucking, sex, set up
            between –

CINDY   Did you hear –

VINCE   You and Nobby No-mates there.

CINDY   Right. First off. His name is not Nobby No-mates.

VINCE   Because –

CINDY   His name is Frank.

VINCE   Are you telling me, real McCoy?

CINDY   And I bet he's got loads of mates!

VINCE   You would have actually.

CINDY   Taxi!

VINCE   Shagged him?

            (CINDY *brazens it out.*)

CINDY   Why not?

            (VINCE *knows what she's talking about.*)

CINDY   Eh Vince? Eh? Why not? Why shouldn't I just go
            out –

VINCE   Okay. Yea.

CINDY   Go to a bar. Pick someone up.

VINCE   I know where you're going with this.

CINDY   Go somewhere. Have sex.

VINCE   I thought we'd had a go at sorting all this out.

CINDY   And then just turn round, and say I'm sorry.

VINCE   I am sorry.

CINDY   No you're not.

VINCE   I am. I've said it fucking loads!

CINDY   Oh yea. You've said it loads.

VINCE   So? Why –

CINDY   But you didn't say it at the time did you?

VINCE   Look . . .

CINDY   Did you?

VINCE   Cindy?

CINDY   Did you?

VINCE   No. I didn't. No.

CINDY   Because you were a bit too pre-occupied coming
            all over her tits.

            (*Not a lot you can say to this.*)

VINCE   I was under a lot of pressure.

CINDY   Obviously not as much as she was!

VINCE   Alright. Fuck it. Yes. I have a problem. There. I've
           said it. My name is Vincent Boyle, and I'm saying
           it to you, here, now, in the middle of the fucking
           street, I have a problem. And the thing is, and I'm
           being genuine here Cindy. I want to sort it out.
           Because, I know, most of the time, I'm like some,
           some, big, helpless kid with it all, because, the
           world is, is, it's like, all it is this big, fucking,
           knock-off sweet shop, full of loads of stuff, that I
           want to, just, see it, want it, have it. I can't help
           myself.

CINDY   Do you know what Vince?

VINCE   It's my nature.

CINDY   If I've heard it once –

VINCE   I've just laid myself on the line there.

           (*They now start shouting over each other.*)

CINDY   I've heard it a million fucking times. It's just
           words. Loads of words that don't mean anything.
           You open your mouth, and they all pour out, along
           with all the bullshit and lies that you–

VINCE   Yea, but this time, I, actually, look, if you just, let
           me say what, fuck's sake. Okay. Alright. Go on.
           Say it. Tell me. Tell me.

           (*We hear this.*)

VINCE   What do I need to do to prove that I'm, I'm
           serious about this.

           (CINDY *thinks.*)

CINDY   Go and see if Frank's alright.

VINCE   What?

CINDY   Go and find him. See if he's okay.

VINCE   Frank? You mean –

CINDY   And say you're sorry.

VINCE   Eh? What for?

CINDY   You beat him up!

VINCE   No. I just said didn't I. I partially winded him.

CINDY   See, you're doing it again. You ask me, I say what I want you to do, and then it never happens. The same old, same old. Here we go again.

(Again they are shouting over each other.)

VINCE   Look, alright. Listen. Listen. I want to say something. Can you. Eh. Will you just hear me out. Cindy? Please. Alright. Listen.

CINDY   Always the same. One lame excuse after another. I'm, I'm, sick of it Vince. Do you hear what I'm saying?

(VINCE suddenly exclaims.)

VINCE   Spain!

(Did CINDY hear this right?)

CINDY   What?

VINCE   Spain!

CINDY   Vince? Did you –

VINCE   Yea. I did.

CINDY   Spain?

VINCE   Yea.

CINDY   What about Spain?

VINCE   Exactly.

CINDY   Eh?

VINCE   I'm not saying we go now, this minute . . .

CINDY   We go to Spain?

VINCE   Yes. Me and you, we. Yea. We. We go to Spain.

CINDY   And do what?

VINCE   Do, whatever, you know, swim. Barbecue. Play
             golf.

CINDY   Play golf?

VINCE   Yea, I know . . .

CINDY   Why would I want to do that?

VINCE   I didn't think that one through . . .

CINDY   I hate golf. Golf's really fucking stupid.

VINCE   Okay, yea, I know, I know you do. But listen, what
             I'm thinking is . . .

CINDY   What?

             (VINCE *takes a moment.*)

VINCE   Prima Dona.

             (*This has a noticeable effect on* CINDY.)

CINDY   Prima Dona?

VINCE   Yea.

CINDY   Vince? Are you –

VINCE   Why not? We've talked about it.

CINDY   Yea, we've talked about it, but –

VINCE   So, let's go for it. Let's –

CINDY   Are you serious Vince?

VINCE   Of course I am. Because, you know, I'm not, I'm
            not just saying stuff here off the top of my head.

CINDY   We'd open the shop? The boutique?

VINCE   Yea.

CINDY   And you'd let me, I –

VINCE   Of course you would.

CINDY   I'd run it?

VINCE   You'd be great.

            (CINDY *takes a moment to think this through.*)

CINDY   But, how –

VINCE   Look. The nightclub. The insurance money. It's
            almost in the bank. We get that, two plane tickets,
            and we're off. Simple as. Just, get out there, and
            fucking grab it. Go for it. Have an adventure. Eh?
            Because . . .

            (CINDY *is giving the whole thing serious
            consideration.*)

VINCE   I love you babe.

CINDY   No, Vince, don't –

VINCE   But I do. I can't help myself.

            (CINDY *struggles, almost frustrated with herself.*)

CINDY   Yea, well, of course, I, yeah, I . . . Vince, but –

VINCE   But what?

CINDY   Are you serious?

VINCE   Yea. I am seriously effing fucking serious. We can
           do this. We'll have all the top, friggin', Jean Paul
           Goatee, beard or whatever his name is, Dolce, and
           whatsit, Vivienne Westwood, Moschino,
           Alexander, Mc, thingy, him, and –

CINDY   McQueen.

VINCE   Him as well. The lot. All of 'em. Whatever you
           say, it's there. And you Cindy, you, listen, right,
           listen, you're the boss, right, because . . .

           (CINDY *is giving serious consideration.*)

VINCE   You'd be absolutely, fucking, astonishingly,
           fucking, amazing. What do you say?

           (CINDY *relents.*)

CINDY   Okay. Yea. Alright. Yea. Why not?

VINCE   Yes! Come here.

           (*They kiss.*)

CINDY   Oh my God. Spain!

VINCE   Because, all this, yea, this is all yesterday all this.

           (VINCE *starts to sing 'Y Viva Espana'. Adapts
           some of the words 'we're all off to sunny Spain /
           Viva Espana / our shop's going to be full of
           Ralph Lorraine.'*)

CINDY   Ralph Lauren.

VINCE   Loads of it.

CINDY   Armani?

VINCE   Even more.

CINDY   Stella McCartney?

VINCE   We'll even get her dad over to cut the ribbon.
               Whatever you want. Just say the label. Like, the,
               eh, what was the, er, the name of, the, ooh, that
               smart little coat I got you that time?

CINDY   A what?

VINCE   The, coat, you remember, with, the, it had a, a trim
               on the –

CINDY   I don't think, er . . .

VINCE   Yea. It was, er, Gucci!

CINDY   Gucci?

VINCE   Si. Gucci.

CINDY   Gucci?

VINCE   Yeah. Gucci.

CINDY   I don't remember you ever buying me a –

VINCE   Actually. Now. Now that I've just said that . . .

CINDY   I'd remember something like that.

VINCE   That was wrong.

CINDY   So if you didn't buy it for me, Vince . . .

VINCE   See, whoa, that's what I'm saying, Cindy whoa –
               sometimes, I get things all mixed up in my head.

CINDY   Who did you buy it for?

VINCE   It's a bit like dyslexia, but with memories.

(GRAEME *has entered.*)

GRAEME   Vince?

CINDY   Who did you buy it for?

GRAEME   Vince?

VINCE   I didn't buy it for anyone, I –

GRAEME   Vince!

VINCE   What? What is it? What are you doing here?

GRAEME   Where have you been? I've been waiting for you at the club for the last hour and a half. As we arranged.

VINCE   Eh?

GRAEME   And it's not as though I haven't got somewhere else to be Vince, because –

VINCE   Look, mate –

GRAEME   I'm supposed to be presenting the after-dinner auction. As we speak.

CINDY   Vince?

VINCE   Yea, okay.

GRAEME   And it's for a tennis racket signed by Tim Henman.

VINCE   Look Graeme. Can you not see I'm –

GRAEME   But the thing is Vince, as I explained at some length in my phone message earlier this evening –

VINCE   I'm a bit busy.

GRAEME   I'm not happy Vince. All this, the phone calls, it's seriously, I'm, it's getting out of hand, and then when he phoned me tonight –

CINDY   What are you doing now?

VINCE   It's nothing, it's –

GRAEME   Nothing? I wouldn't describe this as nothing Vince, because –

CINDY   I thought the club and all that was sorted.

VINCE   It is sorted.

CINDY   Well what's he doing here then?

GRAEME   Because really Vince, all this, it's all getting a bit too . . . eh?

VINCE   Graeme, please, will you just –

GRAEME   Near the knuckles all this, because, I'm not used to this sort of business.

VINCE   I don't need this right now.

GRAEME   And either I want you to do something Vince, or I, basically, I –

CINDY   Fuck this.

VINCE   Eh, whoa, whoa, Cindy, no . . .

CINDY   I'm not standing about whilst you and him have some sort of discussion –

VINCE   We're not discussing anything right, because –

GRAEME   It's more of a shareholder's meeting.

VINCE   What? What the fuck are you talking about now?

GRAEME   I want out, Vince.

VINCE	Want out? No. No way.
CINDY	See, you're doing it again.
VINCE	No, eh, hold on –
CINDY	Because who did you buy it for Vince?
VINCE	Eh? Who did I buy what for?
CINDY	The coat. The little thing, with the trim.
VINCE	I don't know. No. I mean, no one, I –
GRAEME	Vince! Did you hear what I –
VINCE	Yes! Yes, I heard you mate.
GRAEME	Because, frankly Vince, this, it's not my idea of a good night out, this.
VINCE	Well why don't you just fuck off then?
GRAEME	Because I'm not sure if I can keep my mouth shut.
VINCE	Oh. Do you know what?
GRAEME	Yea, what about that eh?
CINDY	Vince?
VINCE	Yeah. Hold on.
GRAEME	Because I'm a man on the edge Vince.
VINCE	Will you –
GRAEME	I could do anything. I'm a coiled spring waiting to go off Vince, because –
VINCE	Shut the fuck up!

(GRAEME *shuts the fuck up.* VINCE *eyeballs him.* CINDY *has left. He turns back to* CINDY *and sees she is gone.*)

VINCE   Oh no. No. No, no, no, no. No. No. Shit. No. Cindy? Cindy?!

(VINCE *struggles with himself, and what to do.* GRAEME *watches. A moment, and then* FRANK *emerges from the hotel. Has just paid for the room.*)

FRANK   Yes, well, next time, I will, yea, I'll read the small print.

(*Puts away his wallet. Turns. Sees* VINCE. *And* GRAEME. VINCE *is all smiles.*)

VINCE   Frank!

(FRANK *is very wary.*)

VINCE   I was just, seriously, I was just thinking about you.

FRANK   Were you?

VINCE   I was mate, yea. You just popped into my head, and I thought –

(FRANK *is wondering who* GRAEME *is.*)

VINCE   And don't worry about him. He's, er . . .

GRAEME   I'm just the accountant.

VINCE   And I was thinking, do you know what, I owe Frank a few explanations.

(VINCE *moves towards* FRANK, *who instinctively moves away.*)

VINCE   Because Cindy, listen, right, Cindy was very adamant that I find you Frank, and we bury the hatchet yeah, and everything will be alright, and then we can go to Spain. What do you say?

(FRANK *runs off.*)

VINCE   Oh, for . . . Frank? Frank!

(VINCE *runs after* FRANK.)

GRAEME   Oh, eh, Vince? What, what are you doing now? Vince? What about all the, with the . . . (GRAEME *thinks.*) Spain?

(GRAEME *follows on.*)

Scene Four

A chase moment. VINCE *pursuing* FRANK. *Burgeoning night life. Soundscape. Neither of them are particularly good at this running thing. The* PREACHER *appears.*

PREACHER   And what we have to remember is, however much we may try, however much we ignore these things, we cannot run away. We need to stop and listen to the message. There are things that we cannot escape from. Because one day they will catch up with us. It is inevitable. You can only keep running away from the truth for so long.

(*This coincides with the moment of* VINCE *finally catching up with* FRANK.)

VINCE   Frank! Hey. Just, whoa, mate, it's alright, it's, listen, no need to, er, seriously. Just. Take a minute.

(*They both catch their breath.*)

FRANK   What do you want?

VINCE   I understand, naturally you're going be a bit wary, and, oh it's Vince by the way . . .

FRANK   I know.

VINCE   And you're probably thinking –

FRANK   Where's Cindy?

VINCE   That's a good question that Frank. But the thing
            is, at this moment in time, I have no idea.

            (FRANK *is suspicious.*)

VINCE   And I know, Frank, you're just, some, random
            someone, who has somehow got caught up in, in
            all this, this, the Vince and Cindy, fucking,
            cabaret, showtime, and believe me Frank, I know,
            sometimes, she does behave like a, proper live
            wire fruit and nut basket job, but –

FRANK   Say that again. She's a lunatic!

VINCE   Thing is Frank. I can say something like that, but
            when you say it –

            (VINCE *pulls himself back from losing his temper.*)

VINCE   Sorry mate. Apologies. I'm just a bit, you know
            what I mean, strung out by it all. So. As I was
            saying.

            (VINCE *looks to* FRANK.)

VINCE   Let me buy you a drink.

FRANK   What?

VINCE   I'm not saying make a night of it.

FRANK   Er . . .

VINCE   Please Frank, I'm –

FRANK   I don't think so. No.

VINCE   I've just said please –

FRANK   I know you have.

VINCE   Don't reject me then.

FRANK   I'm not rejecting you.

VINCE   What are you doing then?

FRANK   I'm just saying, I don't want to go for a drink with
             you.

VINCE   Come on Frank.

             (VINCE *goes to touch* FRANK.)

FRANK   Look, did you not –

VINCE   Frank? Mate?

FRANK   No. Just, leave me alone.

VINCE   I know you're upset.

FRANK   Fuck off!

             (VINCE *has a thought.*)

VINCE   Okay. Alright mate. Go on then. If that's what you
             need to do.

             (VINCE *opens himself up. He is asking* FRANK *to hit
             him.*)

VINCE   Have a pop.

FRANK   What?

VINCE   Get it out your system.

             (FRANK *is bit confused by this.*)

VINCE   But stay away from the face.

FRANK   Sorry? But, are you. You're not serious?

VINCE   Revenge Frank. You know you want to.

FRANK   No, I don't.

VINCE   Yes you do.

FRANK   I don't. Why would I –

VINCE   Hit me Frank.

FRANK   No.

VINCE   Just do it.

FRANK   Sorry, but I don't think anything was ever solved
            by –

VINCE   Hit me.

FRANK   No!

VINCE   Jesus H, fucking, Corbett Frank. I'm spitting
            humble pie here.

FRANK   Is this a set up? Because –

VINCE   You're just a big friggin' bottler aren't you?

FRANK   No, I'm just –

VINCE   A sad fucking loser.

FRANK   No. I'm not.

VINCE   It's written all over you.

FRANK   Stop saying that!

VINCE   Hit me then.

FRANK   No!

VINCE   Why not?

FRANK   I've just said haven't I. It's because –

VINCE   Is it because you're such a sad fucking loser?

             (FRANK *throws a punch.* VINCE *instinctively reacts*
             by throwing one back. FRANK *falls to the ground.*
             VINCE *immediately regrets what he's done.*)

VINCE   Oh, no. No, no, no, no, no, no, no. Frank. No. Why
             did you do that?

FRANK   You said I could hit you.

VINCE   I know, but –

FRANK   Have a pop. That's what you said.

VINCE   I wasn't expecting you to –

             (VINCE *is very frustrated.* GRAEME *enters, having*
             followed on. Out of breath.)

GRAEME   Look Vince, there's something I want to clear up.
             (*He notices* FRANK.) What have you done now?

FRANK   He said I could hit him.

             (*A police siren.*)

VINCE   Oh shit!

             (*An explosion of sound and light. A karaoke bar.*
             Somebody singing the chorus of 'Tubthumping' –
             'I get knocked down/I get up again, etc'. An
             image of the three women from the hen party
             previous. A drinking game. MAUREEN *drinks. It is*
             obviously a shock to her system. But she is
             enjoying herself. KELLY *downs several shots in*
             rapid succession. And then . . .)

Scene Five

The burnt-out interior of a nightclub. An office of some sort.
FRANK *sits, nursing his injury.* VINCE *emerges from an*
underground cellar holding a bottle of something strong.
GRAEME *sits there as well.*

VINCE   Here we go. Yea. Knew it was down there
             somewhere. This'll smooth out the edges.

             (VINCE *enters the office. Places bottle down.*)

VINCE   There we go. Look at that.

             (VINCE *finds some glasses.* FRANK *stands to leave.*)

VINCE   Whoa, eh, Frank? What are you doing? I thought
             we said, you know, look I've found the bottle and
             everything. Look.

             (FRANK *doesn't answer.*)

VINCE   Because, listen mate, listen, I am sorry about what
             happened just then, and, I do, I feel rotten bad
             about it. Yea? So what I'm saying is, let's have a
             double-quick snifter, you go home, say no more,
             no harm done.

             (FRANK *considers.*)

VINCE   Couple of minutes? Eh? That's all.

             (FRANK *sits back down.*)

VINCE   Thank you Frank. Thank you.

             (VINCE *starts to pour out some very healthy*
             measures. GRAEME *makes his move.*)

GRAEME   Look Vince, whilst you're doing that –

VINCE   Not now mate.

GRAEME   But Vince, it's like I said, I'm –

VINCE   I'm having a drink with Frank.

GRAEME   Yea, but –

VINCE   I'm having a drink with Frank.

    (*Point made.* GRAEME *backs off.*)

VINCE   Do you want one?

GRAEME   No. I'm driving.

VINCE   Right. So. Frank? Frankie, Frank-o, Frankie boy.

    (*Awkward silence.*)

VINCE   So, I, er, so, I don't know anything about you do I Frank?

FRANK   What? You mean –

VINCE   Nine to five mate. What is it you actually do?

FRANK   I'm a postman.

VINCE   Okay. That's, yea, postman. That's . . . I like that Frank.

    (FRANK *doesn't reply.*)

VINCE   Important job that, although I suppose it's, er, not what it was. Eh? You know, like back in the day. Because, when was the last time anyone sent a letter. Postcard maybe, but . . .

    (FRANK *still doesn't say anything.*)

VINCE   But postmen, we're always going need the postman aren't we. Eh?

    (*Awkward.*)

VINCE	So Frank. How long you, er, you been doing that then?
FRANK	Nineteen years.
VINCE	Bloody hell. That's –
FRANK	Thereabouts.
VINCE	Staying power that is mate.
FRANK	Although I'm mostly sorting office these days.
VINCE	Are you?
FRANK	I am. Yea. You know, because I, well, I – I had a bit of trouble with my feet.
VINCE	Did you mate?
FRANK	Yea, I did. Yea.

(*Awkward.* GRAEME *steps in.*)

GRAEME	Look Vince –
VINCE	I'm talking to Frank.
GRAEME	I know you are Vince, but –
VINCE	I am talking to Frank.

(GRAEME *takes this.*)

GRAEME	Okay. You, er, you do that. I'll just, yea, you, you talk to Frank.

(GRAEME *sits back down. But he immediately gets up and starts pacing about.*)

VINCE	So, Frank, what we were, er, what we were, saying there. So, so, postman. Right. Nineteen years. That's, er, look, will you just stop wearing a hole in the fucking carpet like that?

GRAEME   But Vince –

VINCE   All I can see out the corner of my eye is you –

GRAEME   I'm worried sick,

VINCE   Well. Stop worrying then. How many times? There
          is nothing, nothing to worry about.

          (GRAEME, *not hugely impressed with this as
          advice, sits down. Starts to get worked up.*)

GRAEME   Okay. Yea. Stop worrying? Right. That's, yea,
          that's, easy. Just like that. Stop worrying. Why
          didn't I ever think of that? Of course. Fantastic,
          really, yea, brilliant piece of advice that.

VINCE   Yea, alright mate. We get the point.

GRAEME   If only you'd said something earlier Vince, then,
          yea, there wouldn't be a problem. There was a
          problem. Now there isn't a problem.

VINCE   Alright.

GRAEME   Because Vince said, in the face of all the evidence,
          that there was nothing, his emphasis, nothing to
          worry about.

VINCE   Sorry about this, Frank.

GRAEME   And who exactly is Frank? I mean, I'm sorry Vince,
          but, how come, suddenly, how come I'm sitting
          here with some fellar called Frank going on about
          his feet. I mean –

VINCE   Come here . . .

FRANK   Actually I think –

VINCE   No, Frank. We're having a drink. Sit down.

(FRANK *sits back down.* VINCE *pulls* GRAEME *over to one side.* VINCE'S *mobile starts flashing.*)

GRAEME   I'm sorry Vince. I'm sorry. It's just –

VINCE   Will you stop flapping about!

GRAEME   It's just I've never been involved in anything like this.

VINCE   So, look –

GRAEME   Because he rang me up again tonight Vince.

VINCE   No.

GRAEME   Yes. He did. It was him. The, him, you know, the –

FRANK   Vince?

GRAEME   The man who, we, employed on a very casual basis to do something for us. If you know what I mean.

            (GRAEME *gestures, indicating the burnt state of the nightclub.*)

VINCE   And I know you say he's just doing it to me because I'm the weak one.

FRANK   Vince?

GRAEME   But he puts on a bit of a voice as well. 'I want the money Graeme. And I know where you live'.

FRANK   Vince!

VINCE   What is it?

FRANK   It's your phone. It's ringing.

            (VINCE *sees the name of who's ringing him. Grabs the phone.*)

VINCE   Cindy. Babe, I love you. Where –

             (*It is not* CINDY.)

VINCE   Oh. Alright Dee. It's you is it. Yea, well, lovely to
             hear from you and all that, but if you could put
             Cindy on that would be, yea, and I'm sure she
             never said that. Because, I, know she didn't. Look,
             can I, yea, just have a word with, yea, well, if I
             could just speak to her. Just speak to Cindy, that
             would be, yea, if, look, if I could just get a fucking
             word in. No. I'm not swearing at you. I'm just,
             swearing. Because that is going happen. Yea it is.
             Yea. Spain. It's not a pipe dream. It's a proper
             business model. Yea. Well, that's your opinion,
             and, yea, that's, yea, look, can I, no, no, that
             won't happen, because, well, fuck you too, Dee.
             Yea, now I am swearing at you. Yea, fuck off. She
             does. Fuck off. Fuck right off. Fu–

             (DEE *hangs up. This phone call obviously gets to*
             VINCE. *He looks vulnerable. Mutters a few things
             to himself. Sits down.* FRANK *stands to leave.*)

VINCE   Eh Frank? What are you doing?

FRANK   The thing is Vince –

VINCE   Don't go mate. I'm hanging on by a thread here.

             (VINCE *looks to* FRANK. *Desperate.*)

VINCE   Please. I need a shoulder.

             (FRANK *sits back down.*)

VINCE   Thank you Frank. Thank you. Means a lot.

             (VINCE *pours them another drink. They sit.*)

FRANK   So, er, I was wondering. What actually happened
             here then?

GRAEME   It burnt down.

VINCE   You ever done anything stupid Frank?

FRANK   What? You mean –

VINCE   Because of a woman. You ever done that?

               (FRANK *doesn't answer.*)

VINCE   Done something, and then you think, why? Why?
               Why the fuck did I just do that? I knew it was a
               bad idea, but I still, I did it. And now, it's screwed
               up everything. You ever done that Frank?

               (FRANK *still doesn't answer.*)

VINCE   Say something Frank. Talk to me.

FRANK   Yea. I have.

VINCE   You have?

FRANK   Yea. I suppose, thinking about it, it was er . . .

VINCE   What was it?

FRANK   What was what?

VINCE   What did you do Frank?

FRANK   Er . . .

VINCE   When you fucked up Frank. What did you do?

               (FRANK *is still reluctant.*)

FRANK   Right. Well, I, er. Are you sure you want to hear
               this?

VINCE   Frank, mate. Share it.

               (FRANK *eventually starts the story.*)

FRANK   Well, this, what happened, it was about a year
           ago. A bit less. And, it was, Carole, and myself,
           that's my wife, ex-wife, it was, a few weeks after
           we, er, we are divorced now, paperwork all signed
           off, but this was just after I'd moved out. And I,
           er, I think it's fair to say, I wasn't in a very good
           space. Mentally, or otherwise.

           (FRANK *collects himself a little bit, and then
           carries on.*)

FRANK   Because, things weren't, I wasn't thinking very
           straight. And, sometimes, well, quite a bit really, I
           would just, I'd find myself getting in the car, and
           I'd just go and keep a low profile outside the
           house. Our house. You know, see what she was up
           to and that.

VINCE   Of course you did.

FRANK   And, well, it wouldn't take a private detective to
           figure it out, but, it was obvious that she, she was
           seeing someone.

VINCE   I knew it. I knew you were going say that.

FRANK   I don't know why I hadn't realised sooner,
           because –

VINCE   What was his name?

FRANK   Dominic.

VINCE   Dominic?

FRANK   Yea.

VINCE   Jesus Christ Frank. It's bad enough being cheated
           on, but then you find out he's called –

FRANK   She met him through the book club.

VINCE   Oh for . . . it gets fucking worse.

FRANK   Yea. So, I, er . . .

VINCE   Did you sort him out?

FRANK   No. I –

VINCE   Did you have a word?

FRANK   Not really. No.

VINCE   But you let him know eh?

FRANK   Sort of . . .

VINCE   What did you do?

FRANK   Well, actually, I, I know this might sound –

VINCE   What did you do Frank?

FRANK   I hid under the bed.

               (VINCE *wasn't expecting* FRANK *to say this*.)

VINCE   You –

FRANK   Yea.

VINCE   Hid under the bed?

FRANK   Yea.

VINCE   Bloody hell Frank, that's a bit –

FRANK   It's like I said. I wasn't thinking very straight.

VINCE   No, sure mate, of course.

FRANK   And I was wearing a mask.

               (*Again* VINCE *wasn't expecting this*.)

VINCE   You, sorry Frank, you –

FRANK   It was one of those, like a skull. Well, it was a
        skull. You know, with the big, bloodshot eye bits.

VINCE   So, hold on –

FRANK   It was just lying about at work. I don't know why,
        but I just –

VINCE   And then what happened?

FRANK   One of his kids walked in. And how was I to, I
        mean, I didn't know he had children.

VINCE   Oh Frank . . .

FRANK   And she was only about four. And you can
        imagine, when she, she came running in, and
        because her eye line was, you know, and there was
        me. Under the bed with my scary mask on.

VINCE   Oh, no.

FRANK   And, obviously, she, er, she . . . she got quite
        upset.

        (*Nobody says anything.*)

FRANK   Thankfully, er, Carole, and Dominic, they, they
        were, I don't think understanding is the right
        word, but they . . . we managed to sort it out,
        you know, without. Calling anyone.

        (FRANK *tries to make some sense of it.*)

FRANK   And, I know, looking back, doing something like
        that, it wasn't . . .

        (*Struggles to find the right word.*)

FRANK   But I was very low. Really. I was, I was seriously
        fed up, you know, not sleeping, not going into
        work somedays, just, all over the place. Not that
        that's an excuse. Because it isn't. I shouldn't have

done it. But I did. I did do it. And I'm not very
proud of myself.

(*A moment, and then carries on.*)

FRANK   But I'm through all that now. There have been a
                 few more dark moments along the way, but I'm,
                 yea, I'm out the other end now. And that's why, I,
                 well, I put myself on the, the internet, web, dating,
                 site. You know, see if anyone else fancies taking
                 me on. Give it a go anyway. Because, well,
                 nothing's ever going happen if you stay in every
                 night is it?

                 (FRANK *realises he's revealed more than he
                 intended.*)

FRANK   Do you know, I . . . I've never told anyone that
                 before.

                 (VINCE *puts a hand on* FRANK'S *shoulder. This is
                 all too much for* GRAEME.)

GRAEME   I'm sorry, but, can, can, somebody, anyone,
                 whoever, please, tell me, please, what, what, what
                 the, flaming, hell, is going on now?

VINCE   Oi.

GRAEME   Because, I'm sitting here, just over there Vince, I
                 don't know if you noticed, but I'm sitting there
                 trying not to worry like what you just said so, but,
                 do you know what Vince, I think maybe all this,
                 it's just one long practical joke, because, what is
                 going on? What actually is going on?

VINCE   Frank has just sat here and said something he's
                 never told anyone.

GRAEME   Yes. He has. Thank you for that Frank. I have no
                 idea who you are, or what you're doing here, but
                 thank you so much for that. Just what the
                 psychiatrist ordered, that was. A story about you

hiding under a bed, and then leaping out on a four
year old girl.

FRANK   Oh, eh, hold on!

VINCE   Now, whoa!

GRAEME   Oh, and do you know what, that's it!

VINCE   What are you doing now?

GRAEME   I've had enough of all this. Where's my briefcase?

VINCE   Will you stop panicking.

GRAEME   I am not panicking Vince, I –

VINCE   You are panicking!

GRAEME   Alright, I am panicking but that's because I've got
            a very good and perfectly valid reason to be
            panicking. Where is my briefcase?

VINCE   You didn't have a briefcase.

GRAEME   I feel lost without my briefcase.

VINCE   Sorry about this Frank.

GRAEME   And now you're talking to Frank again as though
            he, he is someone, who is someone. But he isn't.
            He's a postman. A postman who hides under beds,
            and jumps out on little girls.

FRANK   I didn't jump out on anyone!

VINCE   Will you just behave and sit down.

GRAEME   Well, that, that is easy for you to say Vince, but
            you're not getting phone calls.

VINCE   What have I just said?

GRAEME   In the middle of what was up until that point quite
              an enjoyable charity fund-raiser.

VINCE   Well just ignore him then. Hang up on him.

GRAEME   What?

VINCE   He's nothing. He's just a load of hot wind and
              bullshit anyway.

GRAEME   He's a manic depressive pyromaniac.

VINCE   Exactly.

              (GRAEME *makes a decision.*)

GRAEME   I wish I'd never got involved with you Vince.

VINCE   What you doing now?

GRAEME   And I wish I had never, ever signed that piece of
              paper.

VINCE   Behave. You're just a greedy bastard like the rest
              of us.

GRAEME   Now that Vince, that is exactly the sort of thinking
              I would expect from someone like you. Goodbye.
              Oh, for . . . which way do you go here? I don't
              know where I am.

VINCE   Graeme . . .

GRAEME   Because if I go to prison Vince . . .

VINCE   Oh, hey. Stop that sort of talk.

GRAEME   I don't think I could handle it. They'd smell my
              fear.

VINCE   Nobody's going be smelling anyone's fear,
              because –

GRAEME   I'm going back to the Wirral. Where I belong.

(GRAEME *seems to be heading for the open cellar.*
Turns away from it.)

VINCE   Graeme!

GRAEME   Because, this is bad Vince.

VINCE   Will you just –

GRAEME   No, I won't just anything Vince. Just, you, fuck
             off. And that includes you as well Frank.

             (GRAEME *turns, and falls through the open cellar.*
             Appropriate noises. VINCE *and* FRANK *look on. A*
             moment, and then a manic burst of activity. Noisy.
             A blue siren. This time it's an ambulance. We
             catch a snatch of the PREACHER. *On the mobile*
             phone footage.)

PREACHER   Because hell is real. It's a real place. Oh yes. Don't
             fool yourself by thinking it's something that's
             been made up by other people just to scare you.
             No it is real, and it is here now, in the world. Look
             around. For most of you, even if you don't know it
             yet, you are living in Hell.

                          Scene Six

A and E at a hospital. Very bright in contrast to previous.
FRANK *sits, waiting, next to* STEVIE. STEVIE *has a rather*
irritating high pitched Scouse voice. Signs of him having been
patched up.

STEVIE   Alright mate?

FRANK   Yea. Not bad.

STEVIE   I'm alright.

             (FRANK *doesn't answer. Who is this?*)

STEVIE   It's all a bit quiet at the moment eh? But I'll tell
                you what, this place, few hours' time mate, it's
                carnage. Seriously, you wouldn't know what's
                slapped you in the face.

                (*A scream from* GRAEME, *off.*)

STEVIE   It's like a mad party that's gone really badly
                wrong.

FRANK   Is it?

STEVIE   It's proper mental mayhem dead heavy fan-
                fucking-tastic.

                (FRANK *doesn't answer.*)

STEVIE   Obviously you do get quite a bit of puke and
                blood and that and what have you knocking
                about, but apart from that.

FRANK   Actually I, er, I think I'm going get off.

STEVIE   Alright mate. Be lucky.

                (FRANK *goes to leave.* NURSE *appears, and heads
                him off.*)

NURSE   He won't be long.

FRANK   I'm sorry. Who –

NURSE   The doctor. He just wants a quick word.

FRANK   Right. Nurse, can I just say –

STEVIE   Alright love?

NURSE   So I think it's probably best –

STEVIE   I'm alright.

NURSE   If you just wait here.

FRANK   I think the person you should talk to is outside –

NURSE   And he won't be long.

           (NURSE *exits.*)

FRANK   Because, I don't really know who he is.

STEVIE   You ever had a nurse mate?

FRANK   No, I haven't.

STEVIE   Because, I'm telling you mate, every single, filthy,
           sordid, dirty, depraved, mucky fucking detail you
           have ever heard about nurses, all of it, it's all true.
           Swear to God. Because nurses are –

           (NURSE *re-enters.*)

NURSE   The doctor just said he's going be a few more
           minutes.

STEVIE   Worth every single penny they get.

NURSE   He's waiting for an x-ray.

STEVIE   I was just saying love . . .

NURSE   Were you? That must have been interesting.

FRANK   When you say he's going be a few more minutes –

NURSE   He's on his way.

           (NURSE *sits* FRANK *back down.*)

STEVIE   I was saying that you lot, the nurses, you are the
           most self sacrificing, hard working –

           (NURSE *exits.*)

STEVIE   . . . up for it cock-mad bit of skirt you could ever
           dream of rubbing up against it. Proven scientific
           fact, that.

(VINCE *enters.*)

VINCE   Frank? How's Graeme?

FRANK   I'm not really sure. But the nurse just said –

STEVIE   Alright mate?

VINCE   She said what?

STEVIE   I'm alright.

FRANK   The doctor, he's on his way.

STEVIE   Word of warning though mate –

VINCE   Okay. You stay here.

STEVIE   Don't ever get out of a moving taxi.

VINCE   What?

STEVIE   And I didn't even do it for charity. What am I
            fucking like? Eh?

VINCE   Frank. Stay here.

            (VINCE *exits.* FRANK *stands.* GRAEME *screams.*
            FRANK *sits down.*)

STEVIE   Like a word of advice mate?

FRANK   Not really.

STEVIE   Don't worry about it. Whatever it is. Because –

FRANK   Look –

STEVIE   The simple fact of the truth of the matter is –

            (FRANK *looks close to despair.*)

STEVIE   It probably won't happen. And if it does happen,
         it probably won't be as bad as you thought it was
         going be. And if it is as bad as you thought it was
         going be, why waste the time worrying about it?
         Because you're fucked anyway. Eh? Think about
         it. It makes sense.

         (*A* WOMAN *enters, pursued by a* SECURITY GUARD.
         She carries a bag of water with a goldfish in it.)

WOMAN   Hey, you, get your hands off.

GUARD   Come here.

WOMAN   I'm keeping it. It's mine!

GUARD   You can't have it in the hospital. That's the rule.

WOMAN   No. Get off. This is my goldfish this, and –

GUARD   Give it here, oi.

WOMAN   I won this. And you're not having it. You, fucking
         Nazi paedo bastard!

         (WOMAN *exits, followed by* SECURITY GUARD.)

STEVIE   See mate, this place, because, I'll tell you, come
         half past two, it's, like a cross between a fucking
         freak show and a, a, another mad thing like a freak
         show. But different.

         (WOMAN *with goldfish enters.*)

WOMAN   I'll do you for sexual harrassment you fucking
         animal. Come on Nemo. (*She exits.*)

STEVIE   But the thing is mate, what you have to remember
         above all else, is, you mustn't let anything get in
         between you yourself and a good night out. That
         is above all else, that is the Bible. You know,
         because whatever else is going on, like, eg,
         women, money, even, fucking, climate, the sky's

falling down, all that bollocks, just, don't even go there. Push it under the rug mate, because . . .

(SECURITY GUARD *enters. Has lost the* WOMAN *with the goldfish.*)

GUARD   Oh, for, where has she . . .

STEVIE   Alright mate?

GUARD   No I'm not.

STEVIE   I'm alright.

GUARD   Dickhead.

(SECURITY GUARD *exits.*)

STEVIE   Because, look at me, I've lost what half a pint, bit more, bit less, but no way Jose is that going get in the way of me getting back out there and having it off with my mates big time. Do you know what I'm saying? Because I'm not being depressing here mate, but the thing about the future is –

(FRANK *stands.*)

FRANK   I'm sorry, but I have to go.

STEVIE   We're all going be dead aren't we?

(NURSE *enters.*)

NURSE   He's literally on his way.

FRANK   No, but nurse –

(NURSE *exits. Franks sits back down.*)

STEVIE   So live for the buzz. Like Froggy.

FRANK   Oh, for –

STEVIE   Do you know Froggy?

FRANK   No, I don't.

STEVIE   He looks a bit like a frog.

FRANK   Does he?

STEVIE   Because, once, right. This is a great story this . . .

              (STEVIE *laughs at the memory.* VINCE *enters.*)

VINCE   Frank. Do you know where Trowbridge Street is?

FRANK   Er, yea, it's not far.

STEVIE   He got hold of this six inch nail, and a hammer.

VINCE   Right then. Let's go.

FRANK   No, but, hold on Vince.

STEVIE   Smack, bang, wallop!

FRANK   What about Graeme?

VINCE   He'll be alright.

STEVIE   Right up his fucking nose bit.

FRANK   But the nurse said . . .

STEVIE   Just dangling out it was.

VINCE   Don't worry about the nurse Frank.

STEVIE   He couldn't smell fuck-all for two years, but –

VINCE   Let's go.

STEVIE   It was that funny.

              (VINCE *and* FRANK *have gone.*)

STEVIE   I, literally, shat my kecks. Eh? Do you hear me? I,
            literally . . .

            (STEVIE *sees that he is alone. Self-conscious.*)

STEVIE   Shat my kecks.

            (*Yes he is definitely alone. He stands up.
            Proclaims. Dance beat starts up underneath.*)

STEVIE   Have a good time. All the time.

            (*Holds the moment for a short while as the music
            builds.* STEVIE *imagines he is in the middle of it
            all. Loving it. Having it off big time. Then
            suddenly shifts to a much smaller scene. The
            background noise of a club. The street.* KELLY *is
            on her knees, just having thrown up.* MAUREEN *is
            with her.*)

MAUREEN   That's it Kelly love. You'll be alright. You just got
            a bit over-excited.

            (KELLY *is crying. We can barely make out what
            she's saying.*)

KELLY   I want my Mum.

MAUREEN   What? I'm sorry, I can't make out what –

KELLY   I said, I want –

            (KELLY *starts to retch again.*)

MAUREEN   Okay, look, don't, er, I'm going go and fetch
            something so we can sort you out. Just, stay
            there. .

            (MAUREEN *exits.* VINCE *and* FRANK *enter, on their
            way to wherever it is they're going.*)

FRANK   Look Vince can I just ask –

VINCE   It's this way is it?

FRANK   Yea it is.

VINCE   Keep up Frank.

FRANK   Where are we going?

VINCE   And watch out for the casualties.

KELLY   I want my Mum!

            (*They step round* KELLY. FRANK *notices she is on her own.*)

FRANK   What's that love?

KELLY   I said, I want my Mum.

VINCE   Frank?

FRANK   I can't make out what you're saying there.

VINCE   What are you doing?

KELLY   I want to go home.

FRANK   No, it's just, she seems to be on her own.

VINCE   Someone else'll sort her out.

FRANK   Look, there you go. Just –

            (FRANK *produces a packet of tissues. Unwrapped. Hands them to* KELLY.)

FRANK   Take them. Hold them. That's it.

VINCE   Frank? Will you . . .

FRANK   Alright. I'm coming.

VINCE   Jesus Christ mate, what's your middle name?
            Ghandi?

(They exit as MAUREEN *enters. She has some paper towels.)*

MAUREEN   I don't know where the others have gone, but, I've got a few bits from the ladies so –

*(*MAUREEN *notices the tissues.)*

MAUREEN   Where did you get those from?

KELLY   The man. He –

MAUREEN   Sorry? The what?

KELLY   The lovely man. Ghandi. He gave them to me.

*(*MAUREEN *realises this is a bit of a lost cause.)*

MAUREEN   Look, come on, sit up a little bit. That's it.

*(*MAUREEN *starts to clean up* KELLY'S *face.* KELLY *starts singing. 'Its Raining Men'. A pathetic but touching image.)*

MAUREEN   That's it.

(Then suddenly bursts into full raucous karaoke version on screen.)

Scene Seven

The doorstep of an ordinary house. It belongs to DEE, CINDY'S *sister. She stands there, facing* VINCE, *who has just turned up.* FRANK *stands off, slightly to the side.*

DEE   What the fuck do you want?

VINCE   Look Dee . . .

DEE   I thought I'd made it very fucking clear Vince.

VINCE   I know you did, but –

DEE	Cindy does not want to see you alright?
VINCE	Yea, but Dee –
DEE	What bit of that sentence don't you understand?
VINCE	I'm asking you –
DEE	Well you can ask all you like –
VINCE	Please . . .
DEE	The answer's still fuck off.

(VINCE *makes a move to get into the house.*)

VINCE	I need to see her.
DEE	Hey. What are you, hey, I'll get the fucking dog.
VINCE	Okay. I'm sorry.
DEE	You're bad news you Vince Boyle, because –
VINCE	Yea, alright Dee . . .
DEE	Ever since you rocked up in our Cindy's life –
VINCE	I know you've never –
DEE	It's been one emotional car crash after another.
VINCE	But –
DEE	All the time. Middle of the night. Crying her fucking eyes out.
VINCE	The thing is –
DEE	And who's that?

(DEE *has noticed* FRANK.)

VINCE	That's, er. That's Frank.

FRANK   Alright?

DEE   Frank? What sort of name's that?

FRANK   Well, my Mum and Dad, they were big fans.

DEE   Who of?

FRANK   You know, er, Frank.

DEE   Skinner?

FRANK   No. Sinatra.

VINCE   Look –

DEE   How many times Vince? She doesn't want see you.

VINCE   Yea, she does. I got a text.

DEE   And she's out for the count anyway, so –

VINCE   Eh? How come?

DEE   She took some of them tablets.

VINCE   What tablets?

DEE   The tablets that make you go to fucking sleep.

           (*The faint sound of a very groggy* CINDY. *Inside the house.*)

CINDY   Vince? Vince? Is that you Vince?

VINCE   Cindy? Cindy?

DEE   Oh, hey, what the fuck are you doing up? I
           thought I said –

           (DEE *disappears back inside. An argument.*)

CINDY   Is that Vince? I want to see Vince.

DEE   Go back to bed you. You're in no fit state to, oi –

CINDY   Let me see Vince. I want to see Vince. Vince!

VINCE   Cindy?

CINDY   Vince? Vince!

                (CINDY *stumbles to the door. They see each other.*)

CINDY   Is that you Vince?

VINCE   It's me babe. I'm here for you.

                (CINDY *stumbles further out. They look at each other.*)

CINDY   I'm sorry Vince.

VINCE   So am I.

CINDY   I don't know what happens in my head sometimes.

VINCE   I know, and, I'm sorry. It's, just, we've got to put all this behind us, and –

CINDY   I love you Vince!

                (*The genuineness of this takes* VINCE *by surprise.*)

VINCE   And I love you too babe.

CINDY   I love you loads!

VINCE   Yea, and I love you, I love you loads as well.

                (*They look at each other. Intense.*)

DEE   Jesus fucking Christ!

                (*Full on kiss. Something desperate about it. They hold each other.*)

VINCE   And, nothing's going get in our way now.

CINDY   We're going go to Spain, aren't we Vince? I want to go to Spain.

VINCE   We are. Because this city. It's, look at it, it's full of . . . wankers.

DEE   It takes one to know one.

VINCE   And me and you babe, we're going be different. And look . . .

            (VINCE *steps back to reveal* FRANK.)

CINDY   Is, that –

FRANK   Alright?

CINDY   Frank? What –

VINCE   You know, because, I did like you said. I went off and I found him, and I said, I apologised for all the, what went on, and now, we're, er, well, we're mates now aren't we Frank?

FRANK   Er . . .

VINCE   Aren't we?

FRANK   Yea. I suppose, you could say –

CINDY   I'm so sorry Frank.

FRANK   That's alright.

CINDY   It's just when I saw your picture, and –

FRANK   Well, these things happen don't they.

CINDY   And you have got a lovely face.

VINCE   Hey. Let's get a photo!

CINDY   Yes. Let's get a photo.

FRANK   What?

VINCE   Here you are.

CINDY   Come on Frank.

           (VINCE *has fetched out his mobile, and holds it up to take a photo of the three of them.*)

VINCE   Crowd in mate.

           (*They all look up at* VINCE'S *camera.* FRANK, *between* VINCE *and* CINDY.)

VINCE   Say 'Frank'.

           (FRANK *tries to smile. They exclaim 'Frank'. A flash from the mobile.* CINDY *reacts.*)

CINDY   Oh, God. That was . . .

VINCE   Are you alright babe?

CINDY   Yea, I'm fine, it was just, the light from the –

VINCE   Come on, let's sit you down.

CINDY   I'm alright Vince. I'm okay.

           (CINDY *totters badly. Nearly falls over. Everyone reacts to stop her.*)

VINCE   Whoa, hey, hey, babe, bloody hell, that was, are you alright?

           (CINDY *doesn't answer straight away.*)

CINDY   Yea, I'm okay Vince. But I think, I, maybe. I need to lie down.

VINCE   Yea. Right. Of course, yea. So, er, Dee?

DEE   What?

VINCE   Cindy says she wants to lie down.

DEE   I heard what she said Vince. I'm only fucking
               standing over here. (*Is* DEE *going to take her
               back?*) Go on then. Give her here.

VINCE   Come on babe. Let's get you sorted. There you go.

               (VINCE *walks her back to the door. Before she
               exits.*)

CINDY   We're going go to Spain aren't we Vince?

VINCE   We are. It's written in the stars. It's meant to be.

               (CINDY *exits.* DEE *is not impressed.*)

DEE   It's written in the stars? Will you fuck off.

               (*She shuts the door. Some noise off from* DEE *and*
               CINDY. VINCE *stands, relieved.* FRANK *waits.*)

VINCE   This is it Frank. This is it. Because, eh . . .

               (VINCE *starts to bring his fingers together in a
               clasp.*)

VINCE   Do you know what this is? Eh? Do you know what
               that is?

FRANK   Is it, er, like when you do the thing with the,
               here's the steeple –

VINCE   No Frank. No. This is, this is everything coming
               together. See.

FRANK   Oh. Right. It's just when you were, er . . .

VINCE   Everything coming together.

FRANK	Anyway Vince. That's fantastic, and I'm pleased about that, but I really do think, because look at the time –
VINCE	What you saying here Frank?
FRANK	Well, what I'm saying is Vince . . .
VINCE	You're going get off?
FRANK	Yes. Basically, that's, yea, that's what I'm –
VINCE	Behave.
FRANK	No, honestly Vince, because –
VINCE	We've got to go off and have a celebrate!
FRANK	How exactly, I mean what, when you say celebrate?
VINCE	Everything's coming together Frank. Look.
FRANK	Yea, I know Vince, but –
VINCE	Because if this was Spain –
FRANK	Yea but Vince –
VINCE	They'd just be getting going round about now.
FRANK	They have a siesta built into their day don't they?

(VINCE *looks at* FRANK.)

VINCE	You've been there for me mate.
FRANK	Well, I appreciate that Vince, but –
VINCE	Right. First off.
FRANK	But I haven't really had much choice, have I?
VINCE	Do not be giving me anymore buts.

FRANK   But Vince –

VINCE   What did I just say?

FRANK   You said, don't be giving you, anymore buts.

VINCE   Right.

FRANK   But Vince –

VINCE   I don't believe this!

FRANK   But –

VINCE   No Frank, don't say it. Don't even think about saying it.

               (FRANK *is desperate to say it.*)

VINCE   Don't even think about thinking about saying it.

               (VINCE *holds the moment.*)

VINCE   Because, Frank, me and you, we are going go off, out there, and I am going to show you what the phrase have a good time, all the time in all its pure unadulterated fucking glory, actually means.

               (*Music starts up underneath. 'I Predict A Riot'.*)

VINCE   Because Frankie boy, what was it somebody once said?

FRANK   Er . . .

VINCE   Nothing ever happens if you stay in every night does it?

               (VINCE *proclaims this last line. The music builds and builds. Scene merges with the karaoke bar. As* YOUNG MAN *starts singing they move off.*)

Scene Eight

A mad karaoke bar. Colourful. Nothing cool about it at all.
The words of the song are projected. A YOUNG MAN *sings with*
huge gusto.

VINCE *and* FRANK *enter. The song cuts out just as the chorus is*
about to kick in.

VINCE   Here we are then Frank. You're going love this
            place.

FRANK   Yea, it's, yea. Quite an atmosphere.

VINCE   Because this place, mate, it's full of real people.

            (*A* MAN *dressed as* ELVIS *passes by.*)

ELVIS   Evening Vince.

VINCE   Alright Elvis?

ELVIS   I'll get you lined up.

VINCE   Ta mate. Just give us a nod.

            (ELVIS *exits.*)

VINCE   Okay Frank. Dive in.

            (*They step forward into the main body of the pub.*
            The chorus of 'I Predict A Riot'. The place is
            rocking. FRANK *and* VINCE *heave their way*
            through. MAUREEN *and* JULIE *are also there. Cuts*
            out.)

ELVIS   No, listen, serious point this – I've just said to
            your mate love, you're on a bit after what's his
            face has had a go at defacing Freddie Mercury –
            the powers that are in charge, right, it's always
            been the same, and I'm talking Industrial
            Revolution here, because, all they ever want out
            of us, is for everyone to just behave themselves
            and be good little workers – read your history

books, it's all there – Dancing what love?
Dancing Queen? No never heard of it – and that is
why you get all these scare mongering, what have
you, newspaper stories, and documentaries on the
telly, giving out this message that society is, is,
basically, it's going down the toilet, just because
your average working person likes to go out of a
weekend, dress up, and throw a few drinks their
neck – no mate, I haven't got any Morrissey. Why
not? Because he's a dickhead.

(*Karaoke reprieve. Shift to* MAUREEN, *standing,
waiting for* JULIE *to get back from the bar. A
drunken* YOUNG MAN *approaches her.*)

YOUNG MAN   Alright love. On your own are you?

MAUREEN   Actually, I –

(*He shouts back at his mates, who are obviously
egging him on.*)

YOUNG MAN   Shut up you bunch of wankers.

MAUREEN   My friend's at the bar.

YOUNG MAN   You what?

MAUREEN   I was saying –

YOUNG MAN   Do you want a drink?

MAUREEN   No thanks.

YOUNG MAN   Go on . . .

MAUREEN   No. My mate's already getting me one.

YOUNG MAN   Well, have another one.

MAUREEN   No, honestly –

YOUNG MAN   I want to buy you a drink. Fuck's sake . . .

MAUREEN   No. Thank you. No. Sorry.

            (MAUREEN *starts to move herself away.*)

YOUNG MAN   Alright. Suit yourself. I was only doing it for a bet
            anyway.

            (*He turns back to his mates.*)

YOUNG MAN   Yea, go on then, laugh all you want. Bunch of
            twats.

            (*Karaoke reprieve. Scene shifts to the throng at
            the bar.* VINCE *and* FRANK, *next to* JULIE. *All trying
            to get served.* JULIE *is not having much luck.*)

VINCE   Here mate, over here.

JULIE   You'll be lucky . . .

VINCE   Mate? Excuse me. Hey. Serve the lady she's been
            waiting ages.

            (JULIE *is served.*)

JULIE   Oh right. Gin and tonic, and a white wine. Yea,
            large one. (*To* VINCE.) Ta very much.

VINCE   Anytime love.

JULIE   (*to bar*) Yea. Ice and lemon.

VINCE   This is my mate Frank.

JULIE   Hiya Frank.

FRANK   Alright?

            (ELVIS *speaks over the microphone.*)

ELVIS   Vince? Where's Vince?

VINCE   Here you are. I'm here mate. I'm here.

ELVIS   You're on.

VINCE   Nice one. Come on Frank, let's have you.

FRANK   But what about –

VINCE   Leave it. Alcohol's over-rated anyway.

               (VINCE *turns, dragging* FRANK *away.* MAUREEN
               arrives at bar.)

MAUREEN   Oh thank God for that, there you are!

JULIE   Why? What's up?

MAUREEN   I tell you, I cannot wait to get home tonight.

JULIE   Oh shut up, and enjoy yourself.

               (*Karaoke reprieve. Scene shifts to the podium.*
               VINCE *is there.* FRANK *stands by. Music has
               started. It is 'My Way'. But the Sid Vicious
               version.*)

               'And now the end is near/ And so I face the final
               curtain, ha ha ha/ You can't I'm not a queer/ I'll
               state my case of which I'm certain/ I've lived a life
               that's full/ In each and every highway/ And that
               much more than this/ I did it . . . MY WAY'.

               (*During this,* VINCE *is encouraging* FRANK *to get
               up on stage.*)

VINCE   Here you are Frank. Come on. Get up mate. Do it.

               (FRANK *is very wary. Several bystanders join in
               the encouragement. Until eventually.*)

VINCE   Good man Frank. Go for it.

               (*The punk thrash guitar starts to build.* FRANK
               *starts to sing. Tentative at first, but growing in
               confidence, as the audience egg him on.*)

'Regrets I've had a few/ But then again too few to mention/ I did what I had to do/ I saw it through without exception/ I planned each charted course/ Each careful step along the highway/ And more, much more than this/ I did it . . . MY WAY'.

(FRANK *is astonishingly good at this. Second verse. He really lets go now.*)

'There were times, I'm sure you knew/ When there was, fuck, fuck all else to do/ And through it all, when there was doubt/ I shook it up, and kicked it out/ I faced the wall, and the world/ And did it . . . MY WAY'.

(*Holds the end note. Huge applause.* VINCE *holds up* FRANK'S *arm in victory. Scene shifts to* JULIE *and* MAUREEN. JULIE *is clapping wildly.*)

JULIE   Bloody hell. That was those two fellars standing here before.

MAUREEN   Do you know what? I think I –

JULIE   You what?

MAUREEN   It can't be.

JULIE   More!

(*Scene shifts to* ELVIS.)

ELVIS   Okay, right, thank you. That was fantastic. Well done Vince, and, er, whatever the other fellar was called. And now we've got Brenda – are you there girl? – and 'Bohemian whatsit bollocks'.

(*A very brief snatch. Everyone on stage sings.*)

'Scaramouche/ Scaramouche/ Will you do the fandango/ Thunderbolt and Lightning/Very, very frightening' . . .

(*Then shift to* VINCE *and* FRANK. *They are in the Gents.* VINCE *pulls him into a cubicle.* VINCE *pulls out a packet of cocaine and sets it up.*)

VINCE   Come on Frank, in here. Shut the door.

FRANK   Oh. Vince. That was, bloody hell. I can't begin to say what that was like.

VINCE   I know mate. What happened to you?

FRANK   I don't know Vince. I have no idea. It was as though something just, went off in my head.

VINCE   You were in the zone, mate.

FRANK   Is that what it was? Bloody hell!

VINCE   Right then . . .

FRANK   And now I'm, what is it people say, I'm buzzing Vince, honestly, I . . . Vince?

VINCE   What?

FRANK   What, what's that?

VINCE   What does it look like?

FRANK   Well, it looks like, like, drugs, is what it looks like.

            (VINCE *takes the cocaine.*)

FRANK   And I know this sort of thing goes on, but –

VINCE   All yours Frank.

FRANK   But it's not really my sort of thing.

VINCE   Look mate, you're having a good time aren't you?

FRANK   Yea. Absolutely. It's just –

VINCE   Well, that stuff there will take that good time, and it will make it even, gooder.

FRANK   Really?

VINCE   Yes. Really Frank.

             (FRANK *is thinking about it.*)

FRANK   But Vince, what if, I, you know, because it could go all over the place –

VINCE   Listen, Frank. (*With meaning.*) Do not be such a sad fucking loser all your life.

             (VINCE *holds the moment.*)

VINCE   And I say that as a good friend.

             (FRANK *has a line. Not very well, but he manages it. What is going to happen to him? Music starts up underneath, 'Sweet Dreams'.*)

VINCE   Nice one Frank.

             (*Music builds.*)

VINCE   I'll see you in a minute.

             (VINCE *exits.* FRANK *stands, trying to see if he is actually going to feel anything. Scene shifts to Elvis singing. Then shifts to the narrow corridor leading to the toilets.* MAUREEN *enters, as* FRANK *emerges. They brush against each other.*)

FRANK   Oh. Sorry love.

MAUREEN   That's alright. Frank?

             (FRANK *doesn't recognise* MAUREEN *at first.*)

MAUREEN   It's me. It's, Maureen, you know, from –

FRANK   Oh. Maureen. Oh, hey, bloody hell, it's –

MAUREEN   It's me.

FRANK   It's you.

MAUREEN   Yea, it is.

FRANK   How are you?

MAUREEN   I'm alright. How are you?

FRANK   I'm, yea, I'm, alright as well.

MAUREEN   Was that you singing up there just now?

FRANK   Yea. That was, yea, that was.

MAUREEN   I thought, that bloke looks like Frank, but –

           (*Passer-by.*)

PASSER-BY Fantastic mate.

FRANK   Cheers. Thank you very much.

           (FRANK *is basking in the feedback.* MAUREEN *can't help but be impressed.*)

MAUREEN   So, are you, er, are you still at Dover Street?

FRANK   I am. Yea. Still there. Clinging on. Just.

           (*Another passer-by.*)

PASSER-BY Nice one Frank.

FRANK   Thank you. Cheers. Thank you.

           (*Awkward.*)

MAUREEN   Right, Frank, well, I suppose . . .

FRANK   Actually Maureen, I'm glad I bumped into you like this.

MAUREEN   Why's that Frank?

FRANK   Because, well, I never got a chance to say
           goodbye properly, you know, when you got laid
           off like that .

MAUREEN   I didn't actually get laid off.

FRANK   Of course, I meant –

MAUREEN   I took redundancy.

FRANK   That's what I meant.

MAUREEN   And I'm working in a flower shop now.

FRANK   Oh are you?

MAUREEN   I am, yea.

FRANK   That's fantastic. I love flowers.

MAUREEN   Yea. Well, they're quite hard to dislike.

FRANK   Especially, er, what are they called? The blue, no,
           dahlias. No. Er. Something. Orchids. No. I do like
           orchids, but they weren't the ones I was thinking
           of. My Dad used to plant them on his allotment.
           Er. Anyway. So. What was I saying?

           (*Two* GIRLS *pass by.*)

GIRL   Oh look. It's Frank.

           (*They scream, and run off, laughing.*)

MAUREEN   So, are you, are you some sort of regular here then
           Frank?

FRANK   No. I, no. I've never been here before in my life.

           (MAUREEN *is a bit confused by this.*)

MAUREEN   Right. Well, Frank, it's been –

FRANK   Look Maureen –

MAUREEN   What?

FRANK   About that time, when we, er. I've always wanted
            to apologise.

MAUREEN   Really, there's no need to –

FRANK   You know what time I'm talking about?

MAUREEN   Of course I know what time you're talking about.

FRANK   I wasn't meaning to be rude when I got off like I
            did.

MAUREEN   It was Christmas. We were all a bit tipsy.

FRANK   Because at the time, everything was all a bit . . .

MAUREEN   I know . . .

FRANK   You know, with me and Carole, and –

MAUREEN   It's alright.

FRANK   I was all over the shop. Because, I wouldn't want
            you to, you know, to think I wasn't enjoying
            myself.

            (MAUREEN *is flattered.*)

MAUREEN   And how is all that?

FRANK   Oh. That. Yea. All over and sorted. Divorced.
            And –

MAUREEN   Okay.

FRANK   She's got herself a new fellar.

MAUREEN   Same here.

FRANK   What? You've got yourself a new fellar?

MAUREEN   No. I've got a divorce.

FRANK   Oh. Sorry. I thought –

MAUREEN   I definitely haven't got a new fellar.

FRANK   Fantastic. No. Sorry. I didn't mean to say that. Or I
           didn't mean for it to, to, you know, sound like, as
           if, I was, er, no, that's not, if you see what I'm
           saying . . .

           (MAUREEN *doesn't.*)

FRANK   Look Maureen . . .

MAUREEN   What is it Frank?

FRANK   I was wondering, because, well, it's, been, I mean,
           I've really enjoyed catching up just now, and I
           was wondering, and I know you're out with friends
           tonight, but, next week –

           (VINCE *enters.*)

VINCE   Ah, Frank. There you are.

FRANK   Oh. Vince?

VINCE   What's happening mate? I've been waiting out
           there for you.

FRANK   The thing is, I bumped into Maureen, and –

VINCE   Alright love?

MAUREEN   Hiya.

           (MAUREEN *is instinctively wary.*)

FRANK   We were just catching up, and –

VINCE   There's some people I want you to meet.

FRANK   Well, if you just give me a minute Vince, and –

VINCE   I haven't got a minute Frank.

MAUREEN   Look, I think I'd better –

FRANK   No, Maureen, please, I was just about to say
          something.

MAUREEN   Say what Frank? What is it?

          (FRANK *feels compromised by the presence of*
          VINCE.)

FRANK   I know you're out with friends tonight . . .

MAUREEN   You've said that already.

FRANK   I know, but I'm just recapping.

VINCE   For fuck's sake . . .

FRANK   Maybe. Next week. Would you –

          (DAWN *and* VICKI *enter. Glammed-up uber-Scouse*
          girls on the town.)

VICKI   Eh Vince? What you playing at?

DAWN   I thought we were getting off?

VINCE   We are. I'm just rounding up Frank here.

DAWN   Oh is that Frank?

VICKI   Hiya Frank.

FRANK   Er . . .

DAWN   Vince has been giving us loads of low down on
          you.

FRANK   Has he?

VICKI   Yea. Loads!

MAUREEN   Look Frank, it's been lovely seeing you again –

FRANK   No, Maureen, please, wait . . .

VINCE   So, Frank, let's make tracks eh?

MAUREEN   I can see you're quite busy.

FRANK   This, it's, it's not what it looks like.

DAWN   Come on Frank. We're waiting.

MAUREEN   It's really none of my business.

VINCE   Frank!

(FRANK *turns.*)

FRANK   Look Vince can you just –

MAUREEN   Bye.

FRANK   No Maureen, please, I was just about to –

(MAUREEN *has gone.*)

FRANK   To say something.

(FRANK *stands.*)

VICKI   So are we going go to your place Vince? Or what?

VINCE   Right. Thirty seconds. Wait out there. And then we're off.

DAWN   Oh listen to him.

VICKI   Thirty seconds. Wait out there.

DAWN   It had better not be any longer Vince.

VICKI   Yea. Or else . . .

               (*They exit. Enjoying themselves.*)

VINCE   Okay Frank, what is going on here, eh? Because,
               look mate, is that, or is that not, a couple of life
               size, fucking, 3-D –

               (FRANK *is attempting to interrupt.*)

FRANK   But Vince. Vince? Vince?

VINCE   Eat as much as you like smorgasbord, of an
               exceedingly good time. Or is it not?

FRANK   What about Cindy?

               (VINCE *slightly flips.*)

VINCE   Listen Frank. What happens in Vegas, stays in
               Vegas. And I know we're not in Vegas, but, the
               principle's, the fucking same. Alright?

               (VINCE *stares at* FRANK. *Recovers himself. Steps
               back.*)

VINCE   When you're ready.

               (VINCE *indicates for* FRANK *to leave. He smiles at
               him. Rising dance music. A darker edge to it than
               we've heard before. As* FRANK *is being lead out,
               the* PREACHER *appears.*)

PREACHER   And, above all, do not be tempted. We have to be
               strong. Because the Devil, the Devil knows all the
               tricks. He knows where our weak spots are. He's
               been doing this for thousands of years. Longer.
               And if we let him, he will swallow us up. Like that.
               Because the Devil is everywhere. He was there in
               the very beginning in the Garden of Eden. And he
               is still with us today.

               (*Music builds. Loud.*)

Scene Nine

VINCE'S *apartment. Luxury flat designer bollocks. Overlooks the city. A coffee table.*

VINCE   Right then. At home with Vince. What do you think?

             (*The girls are hugely impressed.*)

VICKI   Oh eh . . .

VINCE   Be honest.

VICKI   This place is fucking boss!

VINCE   Exactly what the estate agent said.

DAWN   Oh, and will you look at the size of that telly!

VINCE   Fifty eight inches.

DAWN   Fucking hell!

VICKI   And hey Dawn, will you look at this.

DAWN   Oh my God!

             (VICKI *and* DAWN *look down on the thronging masses below.*)

VINCE   So Frank? What do you think?

FRANK   Yea. It's, very, it's all quite neutral isn't it.

VICKI   Look at everyone . . .

DAWN   That's mad that.

FRANK   You'd think it might be too much, but, no, it works.

DAWN   Look. There. I know him.

VICKI   Oh my God yea. He's off his fucking lid him.

DAWN   He put that nail up his nose didn't he?

VICKI   Oh, yea. That was fucking hilarious, that!

DAWN   And there's that dickhead who's always hanging about with him.

VINCE   Okay, everyone, get yourselves round this.

              (VINCE *has chopped out an impressive amount of cocaine.*)

DAWN   Oh my God!

VICKI   That is one seriously naughty pile of fucking Charlie that, Vince!

VINCE   Come on mate, sit down –

FRANK   Actually, I –

DAWN   You're being a bit quiet there Frank?

FRANK   Am I?

DAWN   I like quiet men though.

VICKI   Yea. You're lovely you, Frank.

DAWN   You've got a really nice face.

VINCE   And do you know what girls? Frank, tonight, he had his very first snifter of the old hokey-cokey, ever.

DAWN   Is that right Frank?

FRANK   Yea. With Vince. In the toilet.

DAWN   Ah.

VICKI   How sweet is that.

FRANK   Just the one.

DAWN   Yea, but your first line though.

VICKI   It's a special moment.

             (VINCE *hoovers up a line. Reacts.*)

VINCE   Whoa! Eh. Have a bit of that. Fucking, get on it.
             Oh yes.

VICKI   I'll say something about you Vince. You don't half
             put on a smashing spread.

             (VICKI *hoovers up a line. She knows what she's
             doing.*)

VINCE   I try my best. What's the groove pop-pickers?

DAWN   Have you got any Scouse house?

VINCE   Certainly have.

             (*Throbbing, horrible dance music.* DAWN *is now
             snorting a line.*)

VICKI   Woo! Fucking love it.

DAWN   Go on Frank. Your go.

FRANK   Actually, I, er. Will you just keep it there for a
             minute.

VINCE   You alright mate?

FRANK   Yea, I'm great. It's just, er, is there a toilet down
             here?

VINCE   Through there mate.

DAWN   I'll just leave it there for you Frank.

FRANK   Thanks very much.

VINCE   And whilst you're in there Frank, please note, signed photograph of me, myself and Ricky Tomlinson.

FRANK   I'll have a look.

             (FRANK *exits.* VICKI *has another line.*)

VICKI   Oh. That is, that is fucking headbanging, that.

VINCE   Right then. Who wants to have a look at me wet room?

DAWN   Oh you're joking, a wet room!

VICKI   I love wet rooms!

DAWN   I've seen them in loads of magazines.

VINCE   They're very good for opening up the pores apparently.

DAWN   Here, are you being dirty Vince?

VINCE   Behave, I'm talking strictly personal hygiene.

             (VICKI *and* DAWN *look to each other.*)

VICKI   Oh well, alright then.

DAWN   If you insist.

VICKI   Seeing as we're here.

DAWN   What about Frank?

VINCE   Don't worry about him. Come on mate. Get a shift on.

DAWN   Wait till I tell my Mum though, she'll be dead impressed.

VINCE   Give her a bell. Tell her to come to round.

DAWN   She fucking would and all!

             (*They exit. In high spirits.* FRANK *creeps out.*
             VINCE *reappears.*)

VINCE   Frank!

FRANK   What?

VINCE   Get your diving boots on, because it is about to
             kick off!

FRANK   What is?

VINCE   Not sure mate, but whatever it is, it will blow your
             fucking man tits off.

             (VINCE *rubs a bit more cocaine into his gums.*)

VINCE   Get a couple more lines down you. And then get
             your sorry white arse through this door. Is that
             understood?

FRANK   Okay, yea. I'll, do that.

VINCE   And let's get fucking noisy.

             (VINCE *turns up the music. It is now loud. Opens
             door towards wet room.*)

VINCE   He's on his way . . .

             (*Cheering, from off.*)

VINCE   Hurry up.

             (VINCE *exits.* FRANK *considers what to do. Goes to
             leave. Doesn't. Goes back to coffee table. Picks
             up rolled banknote. Goes to leave. Stops. Goes
             back. Sticks bank note up his nostril, and
             prepares to snort.* CINDY *stumbles in. She is very*

> *confused, and unsteady on her feet. She has a key*
> *in her hand. What is going on? Is that Frank?*
> *What's he doing?)*

CINDY   Frank? Frank!?

FRANK   Oh my, Christ Almighty. Shit. Cindy!?

CINDY   What are you doing Frank?

FRANK   Er . . .

> (FRANK *realises bank note is still up his nose.*
> *Removes it.)*

CINDY   Why is it so loud in here?

> (CINDY *stumbles over. Turns music down.)*

CINDY   Where's Vince?

FRANK   He, er, he's having a shower.

> (CINDY *sees all the cocaine.)*

CINDY   Is that all yours Frank?

FRANK   All this? No. It's, er, I thought you were staying
over at your sister's?

CINDY   No. The bitch, she, kicked me out. Wouldn't shut
up. Going on and on. And, it's like, give it a rest
you stupid cow.

FRANK   Actually. I, er, I think . . .

CINDY   It's my life, I'll do with it want I want.

FRANK   I'm going head off. So –

> (VINCE *enters.)*

VINCE   Come on Frank, what the fuck is happening now?
We're –

(VINCE *sees* CINDY. *She is not at all steady on her feet.*)

VINCE Oh eh, oh, Jesus, what the, Cindy!

CINDY Vince?

VINCE How the, whoa, it's you. It's –

CINDY I love you Vince!

VINCE Right.

CINDY Let's go to Spain . . .

VINCE You what?

CINDY Now. Let's –

VINCE I thought you took all those tablets that make you go to sleep?

CINDY Well, I took some others that don't. Yay.

(CINDY *celebrates at this, and as a result, totters back.*)

VINCE Hey. Whoa. Come on babe, let's get you –

CINDY I want to go to Spain Vince.

VINCE Right. Yea. Now, eh, do you know what, that, that is great idea. Let's go now. This minute. Let's, yes.

CINDY Yea. We're going go to Spain.

VINCE Frank?

FRANK I'm going say no Vince. Me and hot weather, it's –

VINCE	No Frank. No. I don't want you to come to fucking Spain, I want you to go and see to the shower, because –
FRANK	Oh. Right.
VINCE	I think I might have left it running.
FRANK	I see what you're saying. You leave that with me.
VINCE	Good man Frank. Right. Let's. Let's go to Spain.
CINDY	Yes.

(*Just as they about to depart,* DAWN *enters.*)

DAWN	Hey Vince. What are you doing now? I thought –

(*A moment.*)

DAWN	. . . you were going to open up our pores.
VINCE	Right. Okay. Can I, first off, I know this must, er, look as though –
CINDY	Who's that?
VINCE	This is, er, this, this, this, is, is . . .
DAWN	Dawn.
VINCE	Yea. This is Dawn, and, er . . .

(VICKI *enters.*)

VICKI	What's going on? Why's it gone all –
VINCE	This is Vicki. And, er . . .
DAWN	At least he remembered your fucking name.
VINCE	And I know, this, er, it must look, I mean, bloody hell, because if I walked in and saw all this –

CINDY   What's going on Vince?

VINCE   I'd be thinking –

CINDY   Who are these 'girls' Vince?

VINCE   And I know this looks bad, but –

CINDY   And where did all this cocaine come from?

VINCE   I can explain . . .

CINDY   Frank?

FRANK   I have no idea. Columbia?

VINCE   Because I did it all for Frank.

(A moment as this sinks in.)

VINCE   I did it all –

CINDY   What?

VINCE   For Frank. All of it. Tell her mate. Go on. Say it.

FRANK   Say what?

CINDY   Stop this Vince.

VINCE   Go on. Say it. Say the, what, it is, why, I, what all this is, here, all this, it's because, because . . .

FRANK   Because of what?

VINCE   Because you're dying Frank. That's it. Yes. It's because . . .

(This has got everyone's attention.)

VINCE   You're dying. And I know, and I'm sorry Frank, I know you didn't want anyone to know, but, there you go, I've fucking said it now. It's out there.

CINDY   Frank is, what? He's dying?

VINCE   Yea. The Doctor, he told him just the other day.

DAWN   Oh no Frank . . .

VICKI   That's fucking bad news that . . .

CINDY   Is this true Frank?

VINCE   I shouldn't have said anything, but –

CINDY   Frank? Is this, what Vince has just said . . .

FRANK   Which bit?

CINDY   The bit about you dying Frank. Is that –

VINCE   Look, Cindy . . .

CINDY   Is it true?

VINCE   You can't just get in someone's face and ask them.

CINDY   Are you dying Frank?

FRANK   Well, I suppose if you think of it long term.

CINDY   Is it true?

FRANK   Yes. Yea. It's, yea, I am. I'm dying.

            (FRANK *is almost as stunned as everyone else that he's just said this.*)

VINCE   So, basically, I said to Frank. Okay mate, dying wish . . .

VICKI   Oh my God!

VINCE   Anything you want.

DAWN   That is so sad . . .

VINCE   Alright. A threesome with two seriously, fucking,
          sexy women. Eh? I can sort that. A shit bucket
          load of cocaine? I can sort that.

CINDY   What of?

VINCE   If that's what you want.

CINDY   What are you dying of Frank?

VINCE   Oh eh, Cindy. Please.

CINDY   Because if you're lying Vince . . .

VINCE   The man is, he's ill, isn't he?

CINDY   But what with?

VINCE   The big, frigging, thing. He's riddled with it.

FRANK   I wouldn't say I was riddled . . .

VINCE   Yea mate, but come on. Please. And I know you
          want to put a brave face on everything, but, the
          truth is Frank, eh, you don't have long do you,
          because, it's just sitting there isn't it, eh, waiting
          to, to grab hold and do what it does, and, I'm
          sorry mate, I'm really sorry, but that's how it is.
          Because you Frank, you, face the facts mate, you,
          you're a dead man walking.

          (VINCE *really goes for this. Has* CINDY *been
          convinced?*)

CINDY   Oh Frank, I –

DAWN   How bad is that?

CINDY   I never realised . . .

VINCE   So girls, is that alright with you?

VICKI   Of course. Yea.

DAWN   I would have done it anyway.

VICKI   You just say what you want us to do Frank . . .

DAWN   I wish we could do a bit more.

VINCE   Believe me, you, are doing more than enough.

CINDY   Oh, and do you know what? I've still got those
            condoms.

VINCE   Oh, hey. Do you hear that Frank?

CINDY   I knew they'd come in handy.

VINCE   Everything is coming together.

DAWN   Oh, ta love.

VICKI   That's really kind, that.

CINDY   They're just in here somewhere . . .

FRANK   No, Cindy, honestly, I –

DAWN   Come on Frank. I really like you, but –

FRANK   What?

DAWN   You've got to use a condom.

CINDY   Here they are.

            (CINDY *produces the condoms. All too much for*
            FRANK.)

FRANK   No. Stop it. No. Look. Cindy, ta very much for the,
            the condoms, but, that won't be necessary
            because, the thing is, look, I'm not dying. I'm
            sorry, but, I'm not riddled with anything, or even,
            feel ill, a bit, or anything, because . . . I do get
            high blood pressure now and then, but as for
            dying, no, sorry, not in the near future. No. Sorry.
            Not dying.

VINCE   (*muttering under his breath*) Fuck's sake . . .

DAWN   Did you tell Vince you were dying?

FRANK   No!

VICKI   That is really fucking twisted.

FRANK   No. I never said that.

DAWN   Why did you say that Frank?

FRANK   No. Listen.

VICKI   That's proper sick that is.

FRANK   I never said that I was –

DAWN   And I really, really liked you Frank.

           (CINDY *launches herself on* VINCE. *Ferocious.
           Slapping, punching, pushing.* VINCE *just stands
           and takes it.* CINDY *eventually runs out of energy,
           and will. She speaks with real emotional
           honesty.*)

CINDY   Why Vince? Why?

           (VINCE *isn't offering an answer.*)

CINDY   Why do you do this to me? Why do you say all
           these things, and never mean a word of it?

VINCE   I do babe, it's –

CINDY   No. Stop it. Shut up. Don't say anything Vince.
           You have no right to say anything. Because all
           you ever do is lie. And I'm so sick of it. And I
           don't want to hear it anymore. Ever again.
           Because, I love you Vince. And you walk all over
           me. And I never, ever, fucking, learn. So, don't. I
           don't want to hear it.

(*Heartfelt. Silence.* CINDY *turns to leave. She walks into the door. Recovers, and then exits. A few seconds pass.*)

VICKI   Look, I think . . .

DAWN   Yea . . .

VICKI   We're going go because, you two –

DAWN   And that includes you Frank –

VICKI   You're both a bit . . .

DAWN   Fucking weird.

(*They exit. At speed.* VINCE *is in a state of shock.* FRANK *is wondering how to get out of this.*)

FRANK   Look Vince, I –

VINCE   Leave her mate. Leave her. Let her go.

(FRANK *doesn't say anything.*)

VINCE   Because do you know what this is? Eh Frank? Do you know what, all that, what happened just then, what that was?

FRANK   Er, no, not really Vince.

VINCE   It's a wake up call, that's what it was. A big, fucking, smell the coffee, do something about it, now, fucking alarm clock. Because, look at me Frank. I'm a mess. I'm a big nancy-boy nobody who thinks he's a somebody. And I have got to seriously sort myself out here.

(VINCE *looks at the cocaine.*)

VINCE   And this is the problem. This stuff here. Eh? Do you see it? Look at it. Just, just, sitting there. Eh? Evil. Just. Don't need it. Move on.

(VINCE *snorts up a line.*)

VINCE   And as you're my witness here Frank . . .

(*Snorts up another line.*)

VINCE   Me, and this stuff. All over. Hasta la vista. Fuck
         off.

(*Snorts up another line.*)

VINCE   Because, seriously, why, why, why would any
         sane human being, ever, ever. Eh? Do you know
         what I'm saying Frank? Because, the sort of stuff
         that's in this most of the time. Petrol. Paint
         stripper. Polyfilla. It's like a, a fucking shopping
         list from B & Q.

(*Snorts up another line.*)

VINCE   And what do we get out of it? A tiny, little, tiny
         bit of a buzz. Talk bollocks for hours on end, and
         then for the next day and a half, all you do is feel
         like shit warmed up in a microwave. It's not big.
         It's not clever. It's not even Charlie most of the
         time. Say no Frank. Just say no.

(*Snorts up another line.*)

VINCE   Do you want some?

FRANK   No thanks.

VINCE   Go on.

FRANK   Honestly Vince . . .

VINCE   Have some. There's fucking loads of it.

FRANK   I don't want any.

VINCE   You're right Frank. Just say no. Why didn't I ever
         think of that? Yes. Say no. Simple. Say no. Say no.

(*He snorts up another line.*)

VINCE   Ok, that was it. That was the last.

(*Snorts another.*)

VINCE   Line.

(*Snorts another.*)

VINCE   Of, cocaine, that will ever.

(*Snorts another.*)

VINCE   Ever.

(*Snorts another.*)

VINCE   Ever.

(*Snorts another. And another. It is now having a very noticeable effect.*)

FRANK   Actually Vince, I think –

VINCE   What? What you saying Frank? What are you fucking saying?

FRANK   I think you might have had enough.

VINCE   You what? Had enough? Are you, saying, are you, Frank, telling me, I, have had enough? Eh? Is that your, fucking, moral platitude you're giving out now, eh, is it? Because, I'll tell you this, I am not my Father's son for nothing. Because, yea, alright, the man was a certified cunt, but if there's one thing he taught me, it was, you can never, ever, ever have enough.

(VINCE *hoovers up every last remaining bit of cocaine.*)

VINCE   There. What do you think of that Frank? Eh? Had enough? You don't know the meaning of the word.

(VINCE *is twitching.*)

VINCE   Okay. Yes. Let's, oh yea, let's, fucking, eh! Let's have it. Do you like seafood Frank?

(*Obvious pain in his chest.*)

VINCE   Eh? Squid. I love squid. All those arms and legs. Yea. In batter. Can't, fucking, yes, beat it.

FRANK   Look Vince. I'm not sure if –

VINCE   I'm alright. I'm okay. Yea. No flies on me mate. Fucking hell yes. No. Eh? Look at me. Frank? Look at me. I'm, yea, baby's on fire. Sorted. Let's go.

(VINCE *collapses.*)

FRANK   Vince? Are you, Vince?!

(*He is not moving.*)

FRANK   Oh no. No. No, no, no, no. Vince? Please, will you. Oh god. Oh shit.

(FRANK *is now shaking* VINCE. *No response.*)

FRANK   Don't just lie there, Vince! Please?

(FRANK *is in a massive panic. He has an idea. He starts to give* VINCE *the kiss of life. He sort of knows what he's doing. Checks for signs of life. Nothing seemingly happening.* GRAEME *enters. He is now wearing a neck brace. He stops abruptly at the sight in front of him.* FRANK *checks for sign of life. Returns to mouth to mouth. Realises* GRAEME *is standing there.*)

GRAEME   Oh. Eh. No. Eh. Because –

FRANK   No, look, Graeme –

GRAEME   What is going on here?

FRANK   It's not what you think it is!

GRAEME   I have no idea what I think it is Frank, because –

FRANK   It's Vince, he –

GRAEME   Yea. I can see it's Vince.

FRANK   You see, what, what happened was –

GRAEME   Have you killed Vince?

FRANK   No!

GRAEME   So why isn't he –

FRANK   He snorted all the cocaine.

GRAEME   What?

FRANK   He –

GRAEME   What cocaine?

FRANK   All the, cocaine. It was –

GRAEME   Where's all this cocaine?

FRANK   No, that's what I'm saying.

GRAEME   I can't see any cocaine Frank.

FRANK   Vince snorted it all. I couldn't stop him. He just kept
             on, just, shoving it up, and, say no Frank, say no,
             and he wouldn't, just, he kept on, and, and I said I
             think you've had enough, and he said, no, never
             have enough, more, more, like this, and then he
             said something about an octopus, and then he fell
             over, and then he. And he doesn't seem to be . . .

             (FRANK *stops*. GRAEME *looks worried.*)

GRAEME   I think we should call an ambulance.

(VINCE *lurches forward. Gasping for breath. As though he's surfacing.*)

VINCE   Agh. Oh. Jeez. Whoa. Oh!

(*Tries to gather himself. Looks around.*)

VINCE   Where am I? Where, where the, where the fuck am I?

FRANK   You're in your flat Vince.

VINCE   Eh?

(VINCE *is hugely disorientated.* FRANK *tries to spell it out.*)

FRANK   You, Vince, you are, see, look about –

VINCE   Frank!

FRANK   Yea that's me.

VINCE   I was. I was out there Frank.

(VINCE *refers to the streets below his flat.*)

VINCE   I was out there. And it was like, this, this, this, mad rush, of everyone, faces. (*Trying to figure out what he's just experienced.*) And it was like, all of us, everyone, we're all, fucking, zombies, just, blah, blah, blah, shouting, and falling over, and shouting again, and again and again, and I could see it, all these, gurning skeletons wearing party hats, trying to kid themselves, and then it hit me Frank. In here. It –

(*As though a shaft of light has entered* VINCE'S *head.*)

VINCE   The truth Frank. It revealed itself. It opened up, there and then –

FRANK   When you say that Vince? You don't mean –

VINCE   We're all fucked.

               (*Holds the moment.*)

VINCE   We. All of us. Everyone. We are all fucked.

               (*Still holds the moment.*)

VINCE   And I'm going go and say it. I'm going go and tell
               it as it is.

GRAEME   I know this is probably not the right time Vince,
               but –

VINCE   We are all fucked.

               (FRANK *and* GRAEME *instinctively step back.* VINCE
               *exits. What on earth has just happened? The
               rising sound of city soundscape. The scene starts
               to merge without the outside.* FRANK *steps
               towards the window, looking down on the city.*)

GRAEME   Okay Frank, listen, we have to go and find him.
               Yea. Because, what was that just then? Because,
               this time, he's lost it. Frank? Do you hear what I'm
               saying?

FRANK   What?

GRAEME   Did you hear what I just said?

FRANK   Yea. Find him. Find Vince.

GRAEME   Right, okay, so, you, see those streets there Frank.
               You do those, and I'll –

               (FRANK *is watching, open-mouthed.*)

GRAEME   Frank?

FRANK   What?

GRAEME   I'm sorry if I'm boring you, but –

FRANK   Is it always like this?

GRAEME   Eh?

FRANK   This. Is it always . . .

GRAEME   What?

FRANK   Like this.

GRAEME   Like what?

FRANK   Like . . . this?

GRAEME   Yea Frank. Yea. It is.

           (*They stand and watch for a moment as the
           soundscape rises.*)

Scene Ten

PREACHER *steps out. The burgeoning maelstrom of late night
city nightlife.* VINCE *appears.*

PREACHER   And if you read through all of the Bible, there at
           the end is a certain Book that lays out before us, it
           tells in graphic detail that out of God's throne
           came thunderings and lightnings and voices. And
           this is the near future. And it's not a comic book.
           This is a real thing. But there is still a chance to be
           saved. You can be saved.

           (VINCE *grabs the* PREACHER'S *small PA and
           microphone.*)

VINCE   Give that here.

PREACHER   No. I'm speaking. I'm just getting to the best bit.

VINCE   Do one.

(VINCE *wrests away the PA and microphone.*
PREACHER *exits. The nightlife rises up a notch. A*
sense of wildness, on the verge of being out of
control.)

VINCE   Okay. Listen.

(*Images of* VINCE *on the backdrop. Weird. Nobody*
is taking any notice.)

VINCE   And I know right, you all think you're having a
good time. Well, big news, fucking, flash headline,
stop press, you're not. None of you are. Even if
you think you are, you're not. Because I know
what you're doing . . . I've seen it. I've stared it in
the eyeballs. And when you get that close, a few
things start unravelling themselves in all their
Technicolour truth.

(*He tries even harder to get people's attention.*)

VINCE   Because, this, it's grotesque this. This is the
dregs. Call this civilisation. This is the arsehole of
the end of the fall-out, this is. We're drowning in a
cesspool of fucking, headless, fucking, hedonism.
Because if this goes on . . . something, it's going
to give. Something's going to happen. Because
there's got to be more to life than this. Wake up.
Do something. Now. Do something better than
this. Anything.

(FRANK *enters.* VINCE *drops the microphone.*)

VINCE   Nobody's listening Frank. None of us. We don't
give a shit. And do you know what? You know
them terrorists? Them, yea. The enemy within? Eh?
Sometimes, I can understand, they come and look
at all this. And I can get it. I can see why they
might want to fucking blow us up. I understand it.
Why they, them, the bad people, why they'd want
to destroy us. Because, we deserve it. It's all
rancid rotten and bad, this. We're all fucked.

FRANK   Vince!

(VINCE *turns, and disappears into the crowds. FRANK goes to follow him, but he is gone. The soundscape rises, a thumping beat underneath it all. A fast and furious collage of images. The noise gets more and more distorted. FRANK is trying to make his way through but is constantly held back. The images continue. Grotesque moments of late night activity. Someone unable to get to their feet. Pissing in a doorway. Vomit. A woman flashing her tits. People leering into the camera.*)

(*As many actors as possible fill the stage. Everything feels on the edge of being out of control. It builds and builds. Activity. FRANK is in the middle of it. A moment when everyone on stage is moving together. It is exhilarating.*)

(*And then a slight wrong move by someone, and everything falls apart. A fight proceeds to break out. Rubbish is being chucked about. A siren. The stage clears. FRANK is caught in the middle of it. He doesn't know which way to go. Then, emerging from the shadows, is a scary mascara-blurred mess. This is CINDY. She wears a wig, and has lost a shoe. Even more off her head than ever.*)

CINDY   Frank? Frank?

(FRANK *turns and sees her. Quite a sight.*)

CINDY   Is that you Frank?

FRANK   Do you know what? I don't need this.

CINDY   I am so sorry Frank.

FRANK   I'm going home.

CINDY   I didn't know what I was doing.

FRANK   Yea, well, hindsight, it's a great thing. Especially
               in, hindsight.

CINDY   Don't go Frank. Please. I –

               (CINDY *totters after him, and spectacularly
               smashes to the ground.*)

CINDY   Oh Frank. Help me. Please. I can't, I can't get up.

               (CINDY *is a truly pathetic sight.* FRANK, *frustrated
               with himself, helps her to her feet.*)

CINDY   Thank you Frank. Thank you. You're so lovely.

FRANK   Look, you'll have to get a taxi.

CINDY   I haven't got any money.

FRANK   Here you are then, look, take this. Take it.

               (FRANK *is giving her a ten pound note. She is
               clinging on him to for dear life.*)

CINDY   No. I can't.

FRANK   Take it.

CINDY   Thank you Frank. I don't know how to thank you.

               (CINDY *gives* FRANK *a full bloodied snog. He tries
               to wrestle himself free.* MAUREEN *and* JULIE *walk
               across the back of the stage, eating something,
               and on their way home.*)

JULIE   Oi, you two. Get a room.

FRANK   Get off!

               (FRANK *pulls* CINDY *away from him.* MAUREEN *sees
               him.* FRANK *sees* MAUREEN. CINDY *still desperately
               clings on to him.*)

MAUREEN   Frank?

FRANK   Oh. Maureen. Er . . .

CINDY   Who's that?

FRANK   Have you, er, you, had a good night then?

MAUREEN   It was alright.

CINDY   Do you want another kiss Frank?

FRANK   Stop it. Will you just, stop.

             (*This doesn't look good.* CINDY *is pawing* FRANK.)

FRANK   This, it's not, it isn't what you think –

MAUREEN   Good night Frank.

             (MAUREEN *and* JULIE *move off, at pace.*)

FRANK   No. Hold on Maureen. Please.

JULIE   Is that the fellar you were saying –

MAUREEN   Yea . . .

JULIE   And that's not . . .

MAUREEN   No. It's someone else.

             (JULIE *looks back. They exit.* FRANK *moves off.*
             CINDY *falls to the floor again.*)

FRANK   I can explain.

CINDY   I'm on the floor again. Where are you Frank? Help
             me.

FRANK   No. Stop it. I've had enough. I'm going home.

             (GRAEME *enters.*)

GRAEME   Frank!

FRANK   No.

GRAEME   There's been a sighting.

FRANK   A what?

GRAEME   Of Vince. I know where he is.

FRANK   And that, what's that got to do with me?

GRAEME   I need you to drive the car.

FRANK   Oh. No. No way.

GRAEME   I can't do it, can I?

CINDY   Did you say Vince? Where's Vince?

GRAEME   Is that, where did she come from?

FRANK   I don't know. Out of a monkey's arse.

             (*Did* FRANK *really say this?*)

FRANK   I don't know why I said that.

GRAEME   Pick her up.

FRANK   Eh?

CINDY   I want to see Vince.

GRAEME   Pick her up.

             (FRANK *can't believe this. He picks her up.*)

GRAEME   Right Frank. There's the keys.

             (GRAEME *throws the keys to* FRANK. *He catches them.*)

FRANK   I'm sorry Graeme. I can't do this.

GRAEME   Eh? Why?

FRANK   I took some drugs. Tonight. I'm, actually, I'm off
            my head.

GRAEME   You seem alright to me.

FRANK   I'm, yea, I'm cooking, I mean steaming. Oh yea.
            Off my trolley. Yea.

            (*During this* STEVIE *has entered. He sees* FRANK.)

STEVIE   Oh. Eh. Look who it isn't. Are you alright mate?

FRANK   Oh no . . .

STEVIE   I'm alright.

GRAEME   Who's that?

STEVIE   Where's the party?

Scene Eleven

GRAEME'S *car.* FRANK *is driving.* STEVIE *and* CINDY *are in the back.*

STEVIE   Thanks for the lift mate.

GRAEME   Keep that foot down Frank.

FRANK   I don't believe I'm doing this.

STEVIE   Have you got any sounds?

FRANK   And why did you say he could come along?

GRAEME   Look Frank . . .

STEVIE   Sounds mate? Eh? Have you got any sounds?

GRAEME   I am under a lot of stress at the moment.

(CINDY *lurches forward.*)

CINDY   I am so sorry Frank.

FRANK   Hey, get off!

GRAEME   And my decision making skills, as a consequence, may suffer.

STEVIE   Mate? Have you got any sounds? Have you?

GRAEME   Look, can you not –

STEVIE   Go on mate. Go on. Put some sounds on mate. Go on. Do it. Do it. Sounds mate. Sounds. We need sounds.

GRAEME   Alright!

             (GRAEME *puts on music. Horrible death metal thrash.*)

FRANK   What's the . . .

STEVIE   Oh, eh. Fucking brilliant mate.

FRANK   What is this?

GRAEME   It's just something I listen to in the car Frank. Helps me forget who I am.

             (*Cut to later in the journey. Thrash metal still underscores the scene.*)

GRAEME   Keep it going Frank.

STEVIE   Hey. You're not going anywhere near the hospital are you?

GRAEME   No we're not.

STEVIE   Because do you know Froggy?

CINDY   Where are we?

FRANK   Look, will you . . . sit her down.

STEVIE   He looks a bit like a frog.

GRAEME   Who does?

FRANK   Don't ask. It's not worth it.

STEVIE   He only went and topped it again tonight eh?

CINDY   I feel sick . . .

STEVIE   You should have been there mate, because, I tell
               you mate, I tell you –

GRAEME   Who is he?

STEVIE   It was fucking hilarious, big-time times fucking
               ten!

FRANK   Will you shut up!

STEVIE   I won't go into graphic detail but it involved right –

GRAEME   Please, don't.

STEVIE   A transvestite, two bricklayers from Poland . . .

GRAEME   Keep going Frank.

STEVIE   Some bird dressed up as Lady Gaga, and a light
               bulb.

GRAEME/   Shut up!
FRANK

               (*Cut to later in the journey. Thrash metal still
               underscores the scene.*)

GRAEME   We're nearly there Frank.

FRANK   Look Graeme, can I ask –

CINDY   I feel sick.

STEVIE   Hey, I think the bird here, she's going to fucking chuck it.

GRAEME   Ignore her. That's it Frank. Keep going . . .

FRANK   I'm doing it aren't I!

GRAEME   Okay Frank, there's no need to raise your voice.

FRANK   Alright, I'm sorry.

            (CINDY *is up and reaching over again.*)

CINDY   I'm going to be sick.

STEVIE   Hey mate, mate, mate, mate, mate . . .

            (CINDY *is now retching.*)

GRAEME   Look, sit her down.

STEVIE   Come on love. Keep it together.

            (CINDY *continues retching.*)

STEVIE   Have you got anything she can use? Here you are. I'll use this.

GRAEME   Oh no, no. Not my briefcase. No!

            (STEVIE *grabs* GRAEME'S *briefcase.* CINDY *is violently sick into it.*)

STEVIE   Go on love. Better out than in.

            (FRANK *and* GRAEME *react to the smell.*)

GRAEME   Oh what?

FRANK   Bloody hell!

GRAEME   Just keep going Frank . . .

STEVIE   You didn't want any of these papers, did you
          mate?

CINDY   Where's Vince?

STEVIE   'Cause they're a bit out of service now if you
          know what I mean.

GRAEME   Keep going Frank. Keep going – keep going – just
          keep going.

FRANK   But Graeme – Graeme – Graeme – Graeme –

GRAEME   Stop the car Frank. Stop the car. Stop. The car.

          (FRANK *stops the car. The sound of an aircraft.*)

Scene Twelve

A piece of wasteland. Near an airport. FRANK, GRAEME *and*
STEVIE.

GRAEME   Vince?

STEVIE   What's going on now then?

GRAEME   Vince?

STEVIE   Where's the party?

GRAEME   Vince!?

          (*An aeroplane flies overhead. Silence.*)

GRAEME   Vince?

FRANK   Look Graeme, are you sure –

VINCE   What?

(VINCE *is dressed in a ridiculous manner, as if heading off to a warm climate. He approaches them.*)

VINCE   They wouldn't let me on the plane. Said I wasn't in a fit state.

(*Another plane flies over.*)

VINCE   Bastards!

(*Daybreak is starting to happen.*)

VINCE   My Dad used to bring me down here. We used to go fishing, just down there.

(*Is this really true?*)

VINCE   We used to catch fish this big. This big.

(*Almost as if* VINCE *is trying to convince himself.*)

STEVIE   That's big, that.

VINCE   And now look at it. It's all gone. It's all, dead. Everything's dead.

(VINCE *pulls out a gun, holds it to his head and pulls the trigger. The safety catch is on.*)

GRAEME   No!

FRANK   Vince!

GRAEME   What are you doing?

VINCE   What's it look like I'm doing?

FRANK   Don't be stupid, Vince.

VINCE   What are you talking about Frank?

FRANK   I know how you feel. Seriously. I do. I, I've been there.

(FRANK *has* VINCE'S *attention.*)

FRANK   I've been there. I was that close. Really. I was.
             And this is only, what, ten months ago. Something
             like that. And I had all the pills. I'd written the
             note. Seriously. Because I couldn't see the point.
             There I was, living in this, this, flat, bedsit, call it
             what you want. And there were these kids.
             Outside. All the time, shouting, saying things.
             Taking the piss. And I'd be coming home, and,
             sitting there, and thinking, look at me, I feel as
             good as dead anyway. My marriage was over and
             done with. My job was pointless and boring. Is
             this it? Is this what it's going be for the rest of my
             life? And I had them there in my hand. I could
             almost taste them. Just there. This close. And as I
             was, I thought, yea, do it now. Do it. Do it. And
             then, say what you want, the phone rang. And I
             was thinking, leave it. Let it ring. It's probably just
             some fellar from India trying to see if I want Sky
             telly or something. But I thought, no idea why, but
             I did. I answered it. And it was, it was my Mother.
             My seventy-eight year-old Mother. And she said,
             'Oh hello Frank, how are you? What are you up
             to?' And, obviously, I didn't say, 'Oh well, funny
             you should ask, I'm seriously thinking of, you
             know, killing myself.' No, I didn't do that. I just . . .
             I started sobbing my fucking heart out. Me, wrong
             side of thirty-eight, and there I am, crying,
             uncontrollably, down the phone, to my arthritic
             Mother. And I could hear her saying, 'Frank, say
             something. What's up, why are you crying?
             Frank? Please. Say something.' And as, I thought,
             I was thinking, I need to pull myself together, she
             said, 'You do know I love you Frank. You do know
             that'. And, something like that, our family, we
             don't say things like that. We might think it, but
             we don't say it. And so, I suppose, because of
             that. What I'm saying, is. Is . . .

(FRANK *reigns himself in a bit.*)

FRANK   Don't kill yourself Vince.

(*Silence.*)

(VINCE *lowers the gun.*)

VINCE   Do you know what Frank?

FRANK   What?

VINCE   You really are a sad fucking loser.

          (FRANK *moves forward and hits* VINCE *in the stomach.* VINCE *falls to the floor.*)

VINCE   Good man Frank. And you stayed away from the face.

          (CINDY *emerges.*)

CINDY   Vince? Vince?

          (VINCE *looks up.*)

VINCE   Cindy?

          (VINCE *stands. They look at each other.*)

CINDY   Are we going go to Spain?

VINCE   Yea. 'Course we are.

          (*They stand looking at each other.*)

VINCE   We're going go to Spain and live happily ever after.

CINDY   You're not lying to me?

VINCE   Babe. Would I ever lie to you?

CINDY   I love you Vince.

VINCE   Let's go home.

(*They start to walk off.*)

GRAEME   So, hold on Vince, hold on. Whoa.

(VINCE *looks back.*)

GRAEME   Is that it? Is that . . . it?

VINCE   Yea. That's it mate. That is it. 'Bye Frank. It's
          been a blast.

(VINCE *and* CINDY *leave.*)

GRAEME   (*shouting after them*) I want out Vince. I want out.
          Do you hear me? I want out.

(GRAEME *turns back.*)

GRAEME   My life never used to be like this. I go to dinner
          parties in Hoylake.

(*He goes to leave.*)

GRAEME   And who are you Frank?

(GRAEME *exits. A moment.*)

STEVIE   Are you alright mate?

(FRANK *looks at him.*)

STEVIE   I'm alright.

(STEVIE *goes to leave. Stops.*)

STEVIE   Have a good time. All the time.

(*He exits.* FRANK *is alone. He is knackered beyond
belief. Sits down. Sun is coming up. A few
stragglers drifting home. He takes out the packet
of posh nuts from the first scene. There is
something of the destitute about him.* MAUREEN
enters. She crosses in front of FRANK.)

FRANK   Maureen? Maureen!

            (*She stops. Sees who it is.*)

MAUREEN   Frank?

FRANK   Yea. It's me. It's Frank.

            (*Neither of them really know what to say.*)

FRANK   So, er, how come you're, er . . .

MAUREEN   Oh. I'm, yea, I'm picking up my kids.

FRANK   Oh. Right.

MAUREEN   Well, their Dad, he, he lives just over there. And
            it's, well, it's all a bit stupid this, but he plays
            football on a Sunday, and, I, er, I owed him a
            favour, and, so, that's why I'm this early. It's
            complicated.

            (*Awkward.*)

MAUREEN   So. How come you're, er . . .

FRANK   That, Maureen, is quite a long story.

            (MAUREEN *can sense not to ask any further.*)

FRANK   Did you have a good night?

MAUREEN   Yea. Not bad. In the end. Well, it was alright. It
            was my mate's niece, she's getting married. And
            I've known her for years. Since she was, oh, about
            four years old. She's twenty-one now. But that's
            nothing is it? What does anyone know about
            anything when you're twenty-one?

FRANK   What do you know about anything anyway? At
            any age?

MAUREEN   I know. We're all just making it up as we go along
            aren't we.

(*The line sits between them.*)

MAUREEN   Have you, er, have you had a good night?

FRANK   You could say that. Although I did think I'd be
            home by half past ten. (R*ealising he had better
            say something*.) And Maureen, can I just say, I
            know you saw me with, er, and then, but, nothing,
            believe me, nothing, went on. Happened. No. I just
            need to say that.

MAUREEN   Are you alright Frank?

FRANK   Yea. Maybe. Not really. I have no idea.

            (FRANK *is obviously struggling.*)

FRANK   You must be thinking, who, who is this flaming
            bloke? Oh look. It's Frank. There's Frank again.
            Just, popping up here, there, and anywhere. Frank.
            What the fuck is he up to now eh?

MAUREEN   Well, I was wondering –

FRANK   Sorry. I'm sorry. I didn't mean to say that.

MAUREEN   Say what?

FRANK   Because I did make a bit of a promise to myself,
            you know, when I came out tonight. No swearing.
            Because, well, you want to make a good
            impression, don't you.

            (FRANK *is very vulnerable.*)

MAUREEN   Are you sure you're alright Frank?

FRANK   Yea. I'm alright. You get off. I'm just getting in
            your way.

MAUREEN   I've got a few minutes.

FRANK   No, really. It's fine. Go on. They'll be waiting for you.

(MAUREEN *waits*.)

FRANK   But, thanks for, er, asking.

MAUREEN   Okay. Well, I, I'll be seeing you.

(MAUREEN *starts to move away*.)

FRANK   But Maureen –

MAUREEN   What is it?

FRANK   Maybe you might fancy a drink sometime. You know?

MAUREEN   A drink?

FRANK   Yea. With me. I didn't mean, in general. I meant –

MAUREEN   I know what you meant Frank.

(*She still doesn't answer*.)

FRANK   So?

MAUREEN   Yea. Of course. That would be, yea. I'd like that.

FRANK   Okay. Right. Fantastic. That's, I'll look forward to that. I'll give you a ring.

(MAUREEN *waits*.)

MAUREEN   Do you want my phone number?

FRANK   Of course. I see what you're saying. Right. Let me just, er, I did have a, er, a pen somewhere. Er. Hold on.

(MAUREEN *takes out a pen, and walks over to him*.)

MAUREEN   Hold out your hand Frank.

(*She writes her number on his hand.*)

FRANK   Okay. Ta for that. I shall action that at an
               appropriate moment.

               (MAUREEN *laughs. She starts to leave.*)

MAUREEN   Oh. And Frank.

FRANK   What's that?

MAUREEN   Go home, and get some sleep.

FRANK   I will. Yea. I'll do that.

               (*They smile at each other. Is this the beginning of
               something?* MAUREEN *exits.* FRANK *waits. He feels
               the sun on his face. He exits.*)

THE END